T0349343

INVESTED IN CRISIS

*Public Sector Pensions
Against the Future*

Tom Fraser

Between the Lines
Toronto

Invested in Crisis
© 2025 Tom Fraser

First published in 2025 by
Between the Lines
401 Richmond Street West, Studio 281
Toronto, Ontario · M5V 3A8 · Canada
1-800-718-7201 · www.btlbooks.com

Library and Archives Canada Cataloguing in Publication
Title: Invested in crisis : public sector pensions against the future
    / Tom Fraser.
Names: Fraser, Tom (Tom C. H.), author.
Description: Includes bibliographical references and index.
Identifiers: Canadiana (print) 2024051114X | Canadiana (ebook)
    20240512049 | ISBN 9781771136693 (softcover) | ISBN
    9781771136709 (EPUB)
Subjects: LCSH: Ontario—Officials and employees—Pensions. |
    LCSH: Pension trusts—Ontario—Management. | LCSH: Pension
    trusts—Investments—Ontario. | CSH: Ontario—Economic conditions—1945-1991. | CSH: Ontario—Economic conditions—1991-
Classification: LCC JL272.Z2 F73 2025 | DDC
    331.25/29135109713—dc23

Cover and text design by DEEVE

Printed in Canada

We acknowledge for their financial support of our publishing activities: the Government of Canada; the Canada Council for the Arts; and the Government of Ontario through the Ontario Arts Council, the Ontario Book Publishers Tax Credit program, and Ontario Creates.

CONTENTS

CONTENTS

ACKNOWLEDGEMENTS

The lifespan of this book began four years ago in Andy Ivaska's grad seminar at Concordia University, a term paper pulled out of an anecdote about New York real estate. From there, it was turned into a thesis proposal through the guidance of Barbara Lorenzkowski and subsequently into a master's thesis with the incredible supervisory support of Steven High. Beyond all else, it was Steven who first put the silly idea in my head that this thesis could be a book.

From this Concordia ecosystem also stemmed the beautiful community of the Deindustrialization and the Politics of Our Time project, who accepted me as an imposter in their subfield, indulged my project at conferences and working groups, and helped me develop the macrolevel theories that scaffold this book.

While at UofT, I learned so much from Ian Radforth, Sean Mills, Matt Farish, Deb Cowen, Cecilia Morgan, Robert Lewis, and Jason Spicer, which has invaluably shaped how I approach research and writing. Conversations with Fred Burrill and Simon Vickers have been vital to how I think about working-class struggle, housing, and trade unionism.

Conversations about pensions and real estate with Alan Walks, Nemoy Lewis, and Sanford Jacoby were deeply helpful in clarifying my thinking and opening up new avenues of analysis I wouldn't have reached otherwise.

Thank you to Cyrus Lewis at *Jacobin* for giving me a place where I could workshop some of the ideas that ended up making it in here. I am especially thankful to Kevin Skerrett and Simon Archer, whose work has informed much of my own and who have been ever-willing to shoot the shit about anything and everything in the pension system.

At Between the Lines, I'm grateful for the constructive and generative editing (and incomprehensible quantities of patience) of Amanda Crocker, as well as the critiques from my two anonymous readers (I have my speculations as to your identities, which I'll keep to myself).

My friends helped in many ways at every stage of this project.

Living in Montreal during COVID lockdowns, the camaraderie of Ed Dunsworth and Vanessa Omaña (and Iggy Dunsworth Omaña, although he won't recall a single second of it) made such a difference in navigating isolation and bad weather, as did the grad school solidarity of Devin Murray, Gabriel Ellison-Scowcroft, and Bree Stuart (with whom I am also tragically bonded through TRAC).

I always appreciated David Baldridge either confirming to me that my ill-informed economics takes were grounded in reality or correcting me when they weren't. About 75 percent of this book was written orally in phone conversations with Neil Kohlmann, who was stupidly patient when I would pin him down to rant about new ideas. Jason Smith and Catherine Brenan took a last minute fieldtrip down to Hudson Yards when I discovered that photos I took in 2019 (unaware they'd end up in a book) were of low quality. Padraic Berting is just a really swell guy and a good friend. Liam Devitt and Gabrielle McLaren were close counsel, the earliest eyes on much of this, and the best grad school pals I could ever ask for. Vivent Les Donalds Sutherlands!

Thank you to my incredible partner Hollis McConkey for your relentless support when the prospect of finishing this book felt like too much for me to stomach, for the mug of Snoopy sitting at the typewriter you gave me when I finished, and for the opportunity to enmesh myself in the shittiness of Thames Water by sheer fluke while you lived in London. I love you so much.

It's impossible to articulate how important my parents and grandparents were over the *longue durée* of this writing process. The period in which this book was in its embryo stage—the peak of COVID in late 2020 and early 2021—was a very difficult time for me and one in which they went above and beyond in their support for me. When the final thesis was completed, my grandmother Nancy Fraser (not the same as the Marxist theorist who is cited frequently throughout this book, much to all our amusement) had my dad print a hard copy so she could annotate it and give me her comments. For two years, every phone call I had with my parents and grandparents included at least one "how's your book going?"

My grandfather Herb Fraser passed away suddenly just as I was finishing my final edits. It saddens me deeply that he never had the chance to hold the book in his hands, but I take tremendous solace from the conversations we had about it, the interest he took, and the enormous love he gave us all. This book is for him.

Mapping the Pension Fund Landscape

Hudson Yards is the largest private real estate development in the history of the United States.[1] A monumental undertaking, the project will ultimately cost US$25 billion,[2] an unprecedented amount even in New York's luxury real estate development economy. The sixteen skyscrapers, located west of Midtown Manhattan on the Hudson River, represent the sinking of almost incomprehensible quantities of capital into the built environment. The scale of the development, when seen from the ground level, is hard to comprehend. The buildings are awe-inspiring in height, and the tallest bears a passing resemblance to Sauron's Dark Tower. In the middle of the complex is an enormous piece of "public art"—a climbable structure called The Vessel that has become a centrepiece of publicity materials and itself a tourist destination.

Planning critic Samuel Stein has labelled Hudson Yards a "monument to private accumulation," a symbol of the vital role real estate has come to play in contemporary capitalism.[3] Looming over Manhattan's gentrified and formerly industrial west side, the glass towers form a "landscape of power," a visible representation of the scale, might, and hegemony of financialized real estate in New York City and beyond.[4] The project was the crown jewel of Mayor Michael Bloomberg's development agenda, the end result of a multidecade process to turn the old railyards into

A few of the glass towers of Hudson Yards. The strange structure in the middle of the complex is The Vessel. Photo by Jason Smith, August 2024.

one of the most lucrative neighbourhoods in the world.[5] In a sense, it is the culmination of New York's *longue durée* transformation "from welfare state to real estate."[6] This transformation has seen New York turn from a city with a strongly working-class character to one of the world's most expensive real estate markets. Hudson Yards is a stone's throw from formerly working-class neighbourhoods that are now playgrounds for the ultrarich.

What makes the Hudson Yards project particularly striking is its ownership, which is seemingly peculiar and yet utterly normal. The development is 50 percent owned by real estate corporation Oxford Properties. Oxford, whose real estate holdings were valued in 2020 at north of $60 billion, is the real estate arm of the Ontario Municipal Employees Retirement System (OMERS), the pension fund

Stuyvesant Town–Peter Cooper Village, a neighbourhood of mid-century high-rises, owned by the consortium of Blackstone and Ivanhoe Cambridge—the real estate subsidiary of the Caisse. Photo taken by author, April 2024.

that pools and invests the retirement savings of over a hundred thousand workers employed by Ontario's municipal governments.[7]

Though unique in scale, Hudson Yards is but one of many real estate developments owned—through their pensions—by Canadian workers. The Hudson Yards megaproject is not OMERS's first major real estate endeavour, nor is it the first time that Canadian pensions have taken an interest in New York's high-end real estate market. While OMERS was building that new neighbourhood on Manhattan's west side, the Caisse de depot et placement du Quebec (or simply "the Caisse")—the fund that invests the contributions of both Quebec's public sector pension plans *and* its contributory state pension plan—went in 50/50 with American private equity firm Blackstone on a preexisting neighbourhood a few miles away on the east side. Stuyvesant Town–Peter Cooper Village, a high-rise community housing over twenty thousand people, was bought for $5.45 billion by Blackstone and the Caisse's real estate subsidiary, Ivanhoe Cambridge, in 2015.[8] Meanwhile, the Ontario Teachers' Pension Plan (OTPP) spent the 2010s expanding the real estate portfolio it holds through subsidiary corporation Cadillac Fairview by over $10 billion.[9]

Real estate returns have become a vital component of the safety net for Canadians' retirement. In the absence of a comprehensive public social insurance scheme, employer-based pensions play a pivotal role in providing for the old age of those workers who have been able to win coverage at the bargaining table, a benefit that was intensely fought for. Pension funds pool the retirement savings of these workers and invest them in capital markets to meet their benefit obligations. And with real estate integrated as a commodity into financial markets, pension investments find their geographical expression in the urban landscape.

This book tells the story of how it came to be that the capacity of hundreds of thousands of Ontario's public sector workers to retire came to depend on real estate and infrastructure. The origins of this, I argue, are in the collision of three processes under the overarching umbrellas of neoliberalization and deindustrialization—the public sector-ization of the labour movement, the restructuring of the postwar welfare state, and the financialization of everyday life. Through these processes, the welfare system of the industrial age has been crucial to the formation and shape of postindustrial capitalism. The result? A system wherein the right to a secure retirement for some—the result of centuries of working-class struggle, unevenly enjoyed—now depends upon the exploitation of many; exploitation that takes the form of skyrocketing rents and crumbling infrastructure.

THE GEOGRAPHY OF PENSION INVESTMENTS

The economic significance of public sector pension funds is perhaps most easily illustrated in terms of their absolute scale. By the end of 2023, the total value of public sector fund assets in Canada was around $1.8 trillion, just shy of the country's total GDP.[10] Their growth has been astonishing and rapid: in 1985, the OTPP (then called the Teachers' Superannuation Fund—the name change is part of the story told in this book), had an asset value of barely over $10 billion, invested exclusively in Ontario government bonds—a generally safer low-return form of financial investment in which the investor takes the form of a creditor and the return-on-investment is basically the interest on that credit. In 1985, OMERS was worth just over $7 billion. Forty years later, the OTPP reported an asset value of $248 billion and OMERS, $128 billion.[11] To put the scale of public sector pension funds into perspective, OTPP and OMERS between them have $376 billion in assets—if you were to combine every single Canadian private sector pension fund into one megafund, its assets would be $456 billion. The major Canadian pension funds—often referred to as the "Maple Eight" in the financial press—have an outsized impact on Canadian capitalism's relationship to the world.

While the public sector pension funds had originally been restricted in their investments to nonmarket domestic holdings, the reforms discussed in this book helped turn them into major players in world finance. Since Statistics Canada began accruing data in the early 1990s, their asset footprint has grown more global with each passing year, with foreign investments now outnumbering domestic ones in fund portfolios. Canadian pension funds hold over $1 trillion in foreign assets under management.[12] The global economic significance of OMERS, the OTPP, and the entire Canadian public sector pension system, however, comes from more than just their sheer size. Part of what makes Canadian funds powerful—and unique—is their particular focus on alternative investments in infrastructure and real estate. In 2012, *The Economist* described Canada's public pension funds as the "Maple revolutionaries," unique in the pension world because of their infrastructure and real estate–heavy investment strategies.[13] The World Bank celebrates it as "the Canadian model," a carefully crafted pension system characterized by independent governance and highly diversified portfolios, which they suggest should be an inspiration to pension funds elsewhere.[14] For both *The Economist* and the World Bank, pension fund investments in the built environment are a key component of Canada's participation in global capitalism. And they are right to highlight these investments. Canadian public sector pension funds own $426 billion in real estate and infrastructure assets, higher than the GDP of Denmark.[15]

Canadian public sector pension funds are some of the largest practitioners of what geographer Brett Christophers calls "rentier capitalism," a model of capital accumulation in which the ownership of assets, rather than the production of commodities, is paramount.[16] By owning an asset, an investor (such as a pension fund) can essentially guarantee income in perpetuity both through the continuous extraction of rent—whether that be tolls on a highway, usage fees for an electrical utility, or, indeed, rent on land use—and by eventually cashing in when the asset's value has appreciated. Neither form of income generation requires much productive work to be done at all, which is why Marxist political economists describe finance as largely engaged in the circulation of "fictitious" capital.[17] Nothing is produced, but pension funds achieve consistently high returns simply through the ownership of their assets.

The usage of real estate as a "storer of value," to quote former United Nations Rapporteur on the Right to Adequate Housing Raquel Rolnik, is a pivotal component of rentier capitalism and the wider financial economy.[18] For OMERS, Hudson Yards basically functions as a grotesquely massive money warehouse. Real estate is integrated into global financial markets, acting in its "pure capitalistic form" as the mediating commodity through which capital circulates.[19] As David Harvey argues, land in this way becomes "in principle no different from similar investments in government debt, stocks and shares of enterprises, consumer debt and so on . . . under such conditions it is treated as a pure financial asset which is bought and sold according to the rent it yields."[20] The consequences of this have been catastrophic. Gentrification has produced incalculable displacement as old industrial landscapes have been transformed into playgrounds for financial speculation.[21] Neighbourhood redevelopment makes the industrial to postindustrial transition physical and visceral.

Pensions, indeed, treat land and improvements as a "pure financial asset." And yet, the extensive literature on the "social investment" of pension funds has engaged little with the particularities of real estate, despite its growing significance to fund portfolios.[22] Critical scholarship on "pension fund capitalism" has tended to prioritize equity investments.[23] Though a broader analysis of pension fund capitalism definitely illuminates the contradiction of "workers' throats being cut with their own money"— the investment of workers' retirement savings in the same companies that are laying them off or busting their union drives—this book suggests that real estate investments have a unique relationship to the labour of their supposed beneficiaries and to a wider radical urban labour politics and therefore must be explored individually.

Pension investments in real estate have exploded since the early 1990s, revealing of a marked shift in both the structure of pension fund capitalism and of the wider political economy of North America. In 1993, Canadian pension funds had $8 billion worth of real estate under their trusteeship—that number is now north of $200 billion.[24] From gentle beginnings with small-scale domestic developments in the mid-1980s, OMERS and the OTPP have grown into some of the big hitters in global luxury real estate; their directly-owned real estate arms, Oxford Properties and Cadillac Fairview, have worldwide footprints worth over $60 billion and $28 billion, respectively.[25] Pension funds are discussed in the financial press like hedge funds and banks—massive investors first and foremost. Their usefulness to finance is far more important than their usefulness to retirees.

The retirement savings of Ontario's public sector workers are crystallized in the built environment, reflected in three dimensions in the form of luxury high-rises, office buildings, and shopping malls. The limiting of a dignified old age to only a segment of the working class on the basis of pension access is linked to the increasing unaffordability of life for working-class people everywhere as a result of financialization. Retirement systems are at the forefront of a political economy reliant upon draining every last penny possible out of everything we need to live and thrive. Pension funds operate as a form of extractive welfare, predicating social insurance upon the exploitation of necessity.

This dynamic produces a sticky situation for Ontario's labour movement. The capacity of workers to compellingly fight for a radical urban politics is inhibited by the dependence of their retirement upon the same forces that are rendering urban life less and less affordable. They are, quite literally, invested in the crisis. The stakes of this book, then, are to understand how this contradiction was formed so we can find a way through which it can be navigated.

PUBLIC SECTOR WORK, HOUSING, AND WELFARE

While their retirement savings connect them to urban land-scapes worldwide, public sector workers are intimately connected to their local urban landscapes through the nature of their labour. The main beneficiaries of the OTPP and OMERS are the workers who make everyday urban life in Ontario possible—the teachers who educate and provide key childcare, the bus drivers who move hundreds of thousands of workers across the city daily, the sanitation workers who clear the streets. Ontario's urban social service network relies upon the labour of their municipal workers, who have earned retirement benefits through their pension funds.

This book conceives of public sector labour, urban land-scapes, and retirement as interrelated under the umbrella of social reproduction theory, a tradition in Marxist feminism that shows how "the production of goods and services and the production of life are part of one integrated process."[26] Marxist feminists have explained how the biological pro-cesses of human survival are embedded within social and economic systems to gain a fuller understanding of how everyday life is both shaped by and shapes the structure of capitalism.[27] While conventional Marxist analyses began with a worker in the workplace and went from there, social reproduction theorists suggest we should ask how the worker got there. Where does the worker live, how does the worker travel to work, what does the worker do today to ensure they are alive and ready to show up at work tomorrow? The work of social reproduction is in large part the work of care, both in its day-to-day household forms and in more structured forms such as education and healthcare. When I discuss "reproduction" and "reproductive labour" in this book, it is referring to the social process of day-to-day survival and the labour required to support that process.

Deindustrialization and its partner-in-arms deunionization meant that the centre of gravity of Canada's labour movement shifted towards public sector workers, a labour force whose work is, by and large, untethered from profit and instead based in welfare services. As wealth in the deindustrialized North is increasingly accumulated through fictitious means—asset valuation arrows steadily moving upwards rather than investments in real production—a new working class has emerged in what we can call the reproductive labour force.[28] Deindustrialization, then, can be thought of as a shift in the primary labour market away from production and towards reproduction, where the main "commodity" being produced is labour, whether it be directly through care work (nursing, teaching, cleaning, etc.) or indirectly through servicing human labour with consumption goods (retail, service, etc.). For these workers, the "commodity" produced is people, and, as the late union activist Jane McAlevey elegantly put it, "the point of production is the community."[29]

The day-to-day reproduction of an individual person depends on access to both labour—the work of caring and servicing—and commodities—shelter, food, medicine, and so on. While the latter have been commodified since the first days of capitalism (indeed, Marx suggests that their commodification is the necessary prerequisite to capitalism), the former have more recently become a terrain of immense profit, as the state-led systems of reproduction that emerged out of the postwar period have been supplanted or permeated by financial capitalism.[30] Some aspects of the welfare state (such as eldercare) have been fully commodified, identified for profit potential by financiers, while others (such as hospitals and education) have remained under state control but have become governed by the guiding logics of the free market. So, although there remains a significant role for the public sector in social reproduction, that role is constantly under siege by finance, constantly under threat of privatization, and managed by the same mentalities as private businesses.

The transformation of public sector pensions into investment funds, totally dependent on the free market for their financing (which I will refer to in this book as "marketization"), is one component of a wider process that has seen the ideology of the free market become altogether pervasive. Under neoliberalism, we have seen a near total penetration of the necessities of day-to-day life by financial capitalism.[31] To put it bluntly, not only is every single aspect of your survival a commodity, but everything you need for survival is subjected to the logics of market exchange.

Housing, perhaps more than anything, embodies this deep relationship between capital accumulation and everyday life. Shelter is, next only to food and water, the most important thing for human survival—no one can live sustainably without it. But housing, as discussed above, is also a commodity, a source of profit for those who own it and who extract rent from it. If we think of wages as representing the value of labour power, they therefore represent the cost of maintaining the worker, one day at a time—that is, by making sure they survive and are sufficiently energetic so as to work. The workers' wage—and the cost of their survival by extension—becomes the landlord's source of rent. One person's life is another person's profit.

Old-age pensions are necessary for the same reason wages are—because workers depend upon income for survival when their reproduction is tied to the market. Comfortable aging depends upon access to the necessities of life, and a pension, therefore, is intended to pay for the continuous reproduction of the self once a worker is no longer in the waged labour force. As the Marsh Report, one of the key research documents undergirding Canada's postwar welfare state, put it, a pension is necessary for "giving help to the aged person in his housing, clothing, and other personal problems."[32] If wages pay for the workers' reproduction during their working life, a pension pays for it after their working life is over.

But as financial actors in an economy where "financial actors redefine social reproduction areas as profit-making areas," pension funds play a huge role in making the workers' life more expensive.[33] The financialized pension fund holds two contradictory forms—one as capital, when it is invested into markets, and the other as welfare, when it exits markets to finance retirement. In its latter form, it pays for reproduction; in the former form, it commodifies it. This is what I call the pension contradiction. Retirement is the collision point containing within it the contradiction between a comfortable aging and the requirements of the pension fund. Aging requires retirement, as the older individual is increasingly unable to work. A pension facilitates retirement by paying for necessities once there is no longer a wage to provide for them. But a pension fund undermines aging by investing in and capitalizing on the unaffordability of those same necessities.

To put it in political-economic terms, comfortable aging relies upon the prioritization of use values while pensions rely upon the prioritization of exchange values, inextricably in tension with one another. With regards to the housing question, this tension is especially pronounced—people need homes to grow old in, while their pensions need property from which to derive value. Adding an extra wrinkle to this is the fact that, in the absence of a pension, property ownership takes on a vital role in the financing of retirement. Those without a pension are doubly hurt—not only do they not have retirement security in the form of a pension, but they struggle to achieve retirement security in the alternative form of asset ownership in part because the pension funds are juicing the property market. In Ontario, where intense housing price inflation has been the norm province-wide since the early 2010s, this tension is especially pronounced.

The private market has always been a vital part of the Canadian welfare system—the socialization of reproduction in the postwar period was only ever partial, with the market remaining dominant, including in both housing and retirement.[34] In English Canada, private homeownership has consistently been the norm, with governmental forays into housing designed merely to buttress the private market.[35] Canada's public retirement system, moreover, was both delayed and limited in its implementation, with state provision only ever designed to supplement employer-based pensions and not to replace them.[36]

That said, capital's takeover of social reproduction has accelerated since the 1970s. With new geographies of production shifting the direct adding of value away from the Global North and towards the Global South, finance has identified human welfare needs as a terrain for accumulation, whether it be through the privatized provision of social services, the financialization of social insurance, or the rise of real estate as a key asset class. The consequences of this have been a protracted crisis of social well-being in deindustrialized countries, best expressed in the form of out-of-control rents, staggering levels of personal debt, and for-profit nursing homes. And on the labour side, those workers who make social welfare possible face downward pressure on wages and benefits as capital seeks to squeeze profits from care.[37]

Struggles over social reproduction are at the core of contemporary labour politics. Fights for fair housing, healthcare, childcare, and eldercare all link those workers whose labour makes survival possible to the struggle for justice in the city.[38] The connection of public sector workers to their communities through networks of care and service has been identified by many union activists as potentially critical to the reinvigoration of the wider labour movement.[39] A teacher has a direct and frequently personal relationship with the parents of their students, a nurse with their patients, a city maintenance worker with their neighbours who use the roads.[40] As a result, they are uniquely positioned to weave labour struggle into a wider fight for a fairer city. But the contradictions of the pension system are a direct obstacle to this—as long as their retirement relies upon the commodification of everyday life, they are held back from being able to fight for a just city.

A LABOUR HISTORY OF PENSIONS

This book is guided by three questions, each of which follows from the other: How did we get here, why is here bad, and how do we get out of here? To answer the first, I trace the development of Ontario's public sector pension funds as market actors alongside the changes in global political economy that produced the modern hypercommodified real estate economy. How did the ability of *some* Canadian workers—those with access to a funded pension—to retire become contingent upon their participation in the financialization of housing and infrastructure? To answer the second, I hope to lay bare the tensions between welfare state restructuring, real estate capitalism, and public sector labour to understand the impacts of the pension system on urban labour politics. And, finally, to answer the third, I ask what is to be done. What, if anything, can workers in Ontario's public sector do to disembed themselves from the processes of housing commodification in which they have become ensnared? How can the tension between a labour movement fighting for fair housing and a pension system that relies upon unfair housing be resolved?

I focus on OMERS and the OTPP in this book for two main reasons, the first practical and the second theoretical. First, narrowing in on only two plans allows me to explore both their portfolios and their histories in greater depth than were I to attempt a wider snapshot of Canada's—or even Ontario's—public sector pensions. An overview of the entire Maple Eight would result in a book significantly larger than this—the Canada Pension Plan Investment Board —commonly known as "CPP Investments"—and the Caisse both warrant a book to themselves. But the OTPP and OMERS are two of the largest employer-based pensions in Canada and the two most important employer-based Canadian funds in terms of influence in global capitalism, and so, when considering scale, I chose to focus in on them specifically. Second, and perhaps more importantly, is that teachers and municipal workers have a unique relationship to their pensions' investments precisely because of the particular geographies of their labour. My analysis in this book, therefore, is in many regards widely applicable to the wider Canadian public sector pension system, but there are also rich particularities associated with the relationship between pensions and the work of *urban scale* public sector workers that I take to be of unique importance.

The world of private capital investment is a

purposefully opaque one, rendering the call to "follow the money" a difficult exercise. This said, I found openings that I used to produce this analysis. First, the 1986–87 Task Force on the Investment of Public Sector Pension Funds produced a considerable archive of documentation, both about the character of Ontario's public sector funds at that moment but also about the process through which they were turned into market investors. Years of back-issues of *Benefits Canada*, a pension industry magazine described in its masthead as "required reading for pension, benefits, and investment executives," gave me insights into both the internal machinations and guiding logics of pension fund investors in Canada. Pension fund portfolios and annual reports helped me trace the development of real estate investments over time.

Chapter 1 provides a history of public sector pension financialization in Ontario. Building on the concept of the "private-public welfare state," which has been usefully developed by welfare scholars, I trace how defined benefit plans became predominantly the domain of public sector workers and how their plans came to imitate the form of their private sector counterparts. I show the rise of a consensus around marketizing pension investments, culminating in reforms to Ontario's pension system that would enable the growth of OMERS and the OTPP into the megafunds we know and love today.

Chapter 2 jointly explores the history of Ontario's municipal workers and their pension funds' increasing embeddedness in the global real estate economy. While OMERS and the OTPP grew into financial behemoths, teachers, bus drivers, sanitary workers, and other fund beneficiaries came increasingly under fire from both provincial and municipal governments that sought to cut costs, discipline labour, and facilitate capital accumulation. At the same time as public sector workers became a major public enemy in the eyes of the state, their pension investments were increasingly directed towards real estate, the driving commodity of neoliberal urbanism. In this chapter, I thus trace simultaneously the urban conflict against both welfare and workers in Ontario from the 1980s to the 2010s and the increasing exposure of OMERS and the OTPP to real estate across the same period of time, attempting to illuminate some of the contradictions that follow from a reproductive labour force being deeply invested in the commodification of everyday life.

Chapter 3 shifts the focus towards infrastructure investments. By exploring the portfolios of OMERS and the OTPP, I show how Canadian pension funds have been active players in the privatization of infrastructure worldwide. Taking a global perspective, I suggest that Canadian pension investments deepen global class stratification by redistributing wealth upwards from colonized populations towards municipal workers in Ontario. Pension fund-ownership of water systems, highways, and land furthers the enclosure of the commons and the dominance of finance over workers in the Global South.

The conclusion reflects on the simultaneous crises of housing and retirement in Ontario, rendered acute by the COVID-19 pandemic. COVID's horrific rampage through private long-term care facilities exposed the stark realities of growing old in the province, despite the scale of its retirement savings. At the same time, the province's housing crisis has hit new heights, with an all-out war against the homeless waged by politicians and police in the summer of 2021. Pension investments tie these two crises together, and activism from public sector workers could be crucial to resolving them both.

In *Social Justice and the City*, David Harvey asked

scholars to write politically, to not simply determine whether or not a given explanatory theory of a social problem is true but rather to ask what would have to change for it to become "*not true*."[41] In this spirit, I ask what conditions would have to change to render retirement's reliance on real estate *not true*. I therefore end by trying to answer the question of what a radical pension politics would look like. Is there a way for the contradiction between pension fund investments and movements for urban justice to be reconciled? Through a brief foray into the history of organized labour's engagement with both the housing and pension questions, I try to articulate the conditions under which pension power could be mobilized towards a decommodified urban landscape.

ONE

Making a Public-Private-Public Welfare State

"I have become aware slowly," opened Jeanne Wellhauser, a rural Ontario teacher, in her letter to the 1986–87 Task Force on the Investment of Public Sector Pension Funds, "that the superannuation money I will be living on for the next few years is woefully inadequate, even though I paid 7.9% of my wages to the fund or, should I say, to the Ontario government." Continuing, she added, "It is my belief that the people who educate this Province's children are grown up enough to manage their own funds. The governments, however, jealously hang onto these funds to run Ontario. I find this immoral."[1]

Wellhauser's frustration that the Teachers' Superannuation Fund (TSF, the precursor to the Ontario Teachers' Pension Plan [OTPP]) was managed by the provincial government was widely shared, not only by her coworkers, but also by financiers, pension managers, and the government itself. In the changing political-economic context of the 1980s, pressure came from multiple directions to transform public sector pensions into market actors, reflecting both a shift towards a financial economy and a retrenchment of the role of private insurance in the welfare system.

When asked to take a historical view of Ontario's pension system, the 2007 Ontario Expert Commission on Pensions determined that it "came not to be a system at all" but rather developed as a messy patchwork of both private and public coverages in which an insufficient state pension is supplemented for some workers by employer-based coverage.[2] This chapter outlines the development of Ontario's pension "system," situating the growth of the Ontario Municipal Employees Retirement System (OMERS) and the OTPP into massive investment funds within the long history of welfare capitalism, deindustrial-ization, and pension reform in the province.

Employer-based pensions developed alongside the state pension system to embed workers' welfare in the marketplace, both by tying their social security to their work status and by funding it through the stock market. Marrying the old ideologies of hard work and savings rooted in the English Poor Laws to a liberal desire to embed social insurance in the marketplace, work-based pensions became a fixture of Ontario's retirement system. Welfare scholars call this sort of arrangement the "private-public welfare state"—a small public welfare state that provides base-level coverage for things like education, health-care, and pension is supplemented by private, (generally) employer-provided insurance schemes that give additional coverage and security.[3] Pensions are a classic component of a private-public welfare state: the Canada Pension Plan and its younger siblings Old Age Security and the Guaranteed Income Supplement are designed to work in concert with employer-based pensions rather than fully support a retiree just on their own.

The employer-based pension system became a defining feature of Ontario's welfare state as it developed through the 1940s and 1950s. Major manufacturing employers in steel and auto had pension plans, which were critical to establishing those jobs as "good jobs." These private pen-sion plans derived their funding from investments in capital markets. In stark contrast, the pension funds for Ontario's growing public sector were entirely government controlled, and their investments were restricted to government bonds, which they were forced to buy at below-market rates. But in the 1970s and 1980s, as private sector pension coverage diminished alongside unionization rates, Ontario's policymakers sought to replicate the private pension system for public sector workers, turning nonmarket funds into major market actors. In 1986, the Ontario provincial government under David Peterson launched the Task Force on the Investment of Public Sector Pension Funds, chaired by public servant Malcolm Rowan, to reassess the regulations governing Ontario's public pensions and oversee the redirection of this capital towards the private market.

All this occurred in parallel to a shift in the political economy of Ontario away from industrial production, opening up significant debates about the province's economic direction. For labour, capital, and the state, the questions of *where, how,* and *under whose control* pensions would be invested had tremendous weight in conversations about Ontario's deindustrial future. The victory of capital in this debate kickstarted OMERS' and the OTPP's enthusiastic entry into the world of finance, setting the foundation for their meteoric rise into two of the world's biggest institutional investors. This history is crucial to understanding our current pension crisis.

GROWING OLD IN ONTARIO

Sixty years before Jeanne Wellhauser was concerned about the sanctity of her pension in the face of potential government raiding, another Ontario teacher felt desperate and afraid about his lack of pension altogether. Seventy-three years old and "struggling for existence daily," a London schoolteacher wrote the Minister of Labour in 1925 pleading for a government pension program to spare him from "the county poor houses . . . those plaguespots of the universe."[4] Even before the Great Depression, elder poverty was endemic in Ontario, with private pension coverage scant and public pension coverage nonexistent.[5] Scant social protections combined with the bodily toll of industrial labour to make aging a truly grim experience in the early twentieth century.

The absence of a government pension and the horrifying spectre of the county poorhouse reflected the hegemony of the Dickensian approach to welfare in Canada. Workers were expected to work hard, save properly, and sire a family to take care of them—if the state had to take on the role of caring for the individual, it would be in punitive fashion. As a result, the first Canadian public pension policy was vigorously means-tested, with government administrators carefully parsing eligibility requirements with a fine-tooth comb. It was intended that a pension be just for those paupers who had failed to either save money properly or sire a sufficient family to take care of them; it was therefore a natural successor to the county poorhouse insofar as it humiliated and punished those in dire need of old-age care.[6]

Looking to reinforce the importance of industriousness and punish those who deviated from it, Canadian policy-makers through the early 1900s insisted that any public pension program be based entirely on contributions from workers rather than through taxation. "Charity," in the form of a pension that was "unearned," would reward laziness. In the 1920s, Prime Minister R. B. Bennett complained that a noncontributory pension would inhibit the development of "habits of thrift and economy," echoing earlier moralizing claims from Wilfrid Laurier that men who were insufficiently thrifty or insufficiently sober did not deserve old-age pensions.[7] A tax-based pension system, they argued, would encourage laziness and ill moral fibre, while a contributory pension would ensure that all were obligated to earn their pension through hard work in their able-bodied life.

The frugal and work-centric approach to public pension provision dovetailed neatly with the nascent and growing employer-based pension system. Private pensions had originated as a corporate strategy to nurture employee loyalty and to help encourage the retirements of workers with high levels of seniority. However, they also fit with the ideological notion that comfort in old age should be reserved for those who had earned it. Insurance programs based in employee contributions would, just like a public contributory scheme, encourage an industrious spirit by rooting welfare in work.

The work-based pension system, with no meaningful or universal pension system to go alongside it, guaranteed that pension coverage was reserved for those workers whose unions had successfully bargained for retirement benefits, leaving a segment of the working class on "islands of security," while others continued to rely on asset-based forms of welfare, the paltry means-tested pensions, and family support.[8] Leonard Marsh, one of the architects of the postwar Canadian welfare state, argued in 1944 that this would be insufficient in comparison to a true state pension system. "Since industrial retirement plans will probably never be extended to even the majority of employees," he wrote, "they cannot be regarded as an alternative to an inclusive state-operated plan."[9]

The whole point of the employer-based pensions, however, was specifically to *prevent* any "inclusive state-operated plan." Employer-welfare programs sought to undercut the appeal of both trade unions and socialism by demonstrating that employers cared about their workers. Although some employer welfare schemes were replaced by the welfare state during the Great Depression and immediate postwar period, this was not the case for pensions.[10] Instead, employer-based pensions continued and grew in the postwar period as the means-test pension remained Canada's only retirement support until the 1950s. This kept a universal public pension at arm's length while building a culture of reliance on employers.

It is not a coincidence that the contemporary legal framework of employer-based pensions and the private-public welfare state in the United States were first codified in the Taft-Hartley Act, more famous for its antilabour and anticommunist provisions. Tying welfare provision to employers, limiting worker control over their own pensions, and (as we will discover) embedding the funding of retirements in private capital markets would serve to deradicalize the US labour movement by giving it a vested interest in the status quo. The aim was to dismantle alternative forms of retirement provision that could potentially build solidarity between the unionized and nonunionized working classes and to sever the bond between workers and the state that had been forged through the New Deal.[11]

While industrial unionism and welfare capitalism had previously been situated in direct opposition to one another, the solidification of employer-based insurance (such as pensions) as a collective bargaining issue in the postwar settlement transformed labour unions from welfare capitalism's opponents into its primary agents. As Gøsta Esping-Andersen puts it, "Once liberalism came to accept the principle of unionism, it was also perfectly capable of extending the idea of individual insurance to collectively bargained social benefits." No longer treated as a bulwark against unionization, employer-based insurance schemes instead became a means of integrating unions into capitalism as unions sought to defend and expand their hard-won benefits.[12] The prime minister who oversaw this process, William Lyon Mackenzie King, himself came from a welfare capitalist background, having spent his professional life working as an industrial relations advisor to the Rockefellers in between stints crafting Canada's employer-leaning labour relations regime.[13] Once union prevention became unfeasible, the strategy shifted to union integration.

As a robust and meaningful public pension system remained absent in the immediate postwar, defined benefit pensions provided security for workers who had won them. A defined benefit (DB) pension is one in which the contributions of workers and employers are pooled, and the onus is on the employer to pay out a predetermined pension. The risk of poor investment performance, therefore, is on the employer, who is obligated to fulfill the pension promise, rather than on the employee.[14]

In the early 1960s, the federal government under Lester B. Pearson made a public pension system a policy priority, laying the groundwork for the Canada Pension Plan (CPP). But while the federal government was working out its CPP plans, the Ontario government in 1963 tabled an act that would make employer-based pensions mandatory for all firms with more than fifteen employees.[15] Such a proposal would have fully entrenched employer-based welfare as the foundation of Ontario's pension system. In its efforts, the provincial government was eagerly backed by both the insurance industry and the Chamber of Commerce, who, for both material and ideological reasons, saw it as a far preferable option to a state system. Indeed, the insurance industry's support for Ontario's proposed Pension Benefits Act was inextricable from its deep opposition to the Pearson government's CPP proposal.[16]

But the CPP was nevertheless successfully implemented in 1965, with the plan that it act as a universal baseline that private pensions could supplement—Ontario, stepping in line, dropped its plans for mandatory employer pensions. A multipillar model of pension provision was codified in which "welfare capitalism in the market and social insurance in the public sector" mutually reinforced one another. The result? A private-public welfare system, similar to that of the US. The basic premise was that if you wanted to retire, you had to work. But if you wanted to retire comfortably, you better hope you were in a union, a status that was deeply gendered in the private sector. When pension access—both employer-based and public—was predicated upon being part of the workforce, the result was lower pension coverage for women, who were often either outside of the paid labour force altogether or in lower-paid, nonunionized employment.[17]

Through the postwar decades, private sector pensions grew and grew, collecting contributions from the growing number of workers who successfully bargained for coverage and investing those contributions in capital markets. And these private pension funds became absolutely crucial to the functioning of capitalism. In the mid-1970s, leading American business philosopher Peter Drucker wrote an influential book called *The Unseen Revolution: How Pension Fund Socialism Came to America* in which he remarked that American workers "owned the means of production" via their pension funds, such was the scale of their investments in the equity of private corporations.[18] Comparing worker "ownership" via their pension funds with state ownership in the USSR, Yugoslavia, and Cuba, he provocatively labelled the United States the world's first truly socialist country. His key point, however, was that the rise of the pension fund had changed the nature of capital formation in the United States as pension investors came to play a pivotal role in capital markets.[19] The phenomenon Drucker had identified in the US was equally substantial in Canada; by 1985, trusteed pension plans held 49.8 percent of Canada's corporate securities, doubled since 1964.[20] Retirement and the success of the stock market were fully intertwined.

The market ideology of pension policy hit its purest form through the financing of employer-based pensions through capital markets. Not only were workers reliant on their employer—rather than the state—for social welfare, but they were dependent on the market for its financing. Through the mid-twentieth century, private sector employer-based pension funds became important players in global capitalism. But public sector pension funds, as we will see, had not yet gotten there.

THE PRIVATE TO PUBLIC PIVOT

As Canada's welfare state apparatus expanded in the postwar period, so too did its public sector labour force, which became a key terrain of labour organizing from the 1950s through to the 1970s. This totally changed the face of organized labour; by 1975, half of Canada's labour movement was employed in the public sectors.[21] The Canadian Union of Public Employees (CUPE), representing workers in the municipal sector across Canada, grew 140 percent in its first decade following its foundation in 1963. A thousand people were joining CUPE a month.[22] The centre of gravity in organized labour was changing—public sector unions grew rapidly while union decline in the private sector, a by-product of deindustrialization, began to set in through the 1970s. This dramatically changed the gender dynamics of the labour movement, as the public sector had a far greater preponderance of women employees than the industrial private sector.

This shift in union coverage from the 1970s onwards was paralleled by a shift in pension coverage away from DB plans and towards what are called defined contribution (DC) plans, a process that really got cooking in the 1980s. In contrast to a DB plan, in a DC plan, workers' and employers' contributions are invested via individual accounts and the worker receives whatever is in that account at the moment of their retirement. The risk of poor investment performance, therefore, falls entirely on the employee—if financial markets crash the day before their retirement, they take the hit.[23] Because DC plans are significantly riskier for retirees than their DB counterparts and are significantly cheaper for and protect the employer, they are more desirable for employers.[24] As union density has declined in the private sector, DC plans have replaced DB ones.[25]

But the attack on private sector pensions was not limited to the rise in DCs, a by-product of declining private sector union density. It was not just that deindustrialization gutted private sector unions—it also directly attacked workers' pensions. American companies through the late 1970s and 1980s took advantage of new funding regulations adopted in the mid-1970s to close plants and cash out of pension obligations by pocketing the surplus.[26] More legislative care was taken in the Canadian context to protect workers from the theft of their pensions but these issues were front of mind for Canadian unionists as plant closures made prenegotiated retirement benefits that had seemed guaranteed seem suddenly ephemeral.[27]

While the dissolution of private pension plans during corporate bankruptcy proceedings in the 1980s captured the attention of both media and the labour movement, a more quiet but equally consequential change was occurring outside the public eye. Running parallel to the shift in the labour movement from private to public sectors was an insistence from multiple stakeholders in the pension industry that public sector funds be run like their private sector counterparts.

Public sector pension coverage, which had originally been rooted in notions of service and loyalty, came to be part of the collective bargaining system, as it was in the private sector.[28] Employer-based pensions—in which the employer was the state—through the twentieth century became almost universal in the public sector, just as pension coverage in the private sector was becoming increasingly patchwork. While private sector pension coverage had been part of a welfare system that reinforced the heteronormative family unit by linking women's access to social security to the employment status and benefits of their husbands, the rise of trade unionism and pension coverage in the growing feminized workforce of the public sector destabilized that traditional family welfare model. Although the employer-based pension system was designed as part of an extremely gendered social welfare system, it outlived it, into a period where that specific social welfare system is, by and large, a thing of the past.

In Canada, 88 percent of public sector workers have pension coverage, compared to just 23 percent in the private sector.[29] Despite the private sector being three times larger than the public sector, there are actually—in raw numbers—more pension plan members in the latter, largely owing to the difference in union density.[30] And, importantly, the megafunds that play critical roles in the capitalist economy are in the public sector—two-thirds of public sector workers are members of funds with over $10 billion in assets.[31] And so the system of employer-based pension provision, designed for the private sector workforce and labelled the private-public welfare state, is now predominantly a public sector phenomenon. In a strange way, it has become a kind of public-private-public welfare state.

The shift in union densities, the rise of private sector DC schemes, and the attacks on private pensions explain why all of Canada's massive pension funds cover public sector workers, not private sector ones. But the pension funds were not always massive—indeed, once, they were far from it. While major private sector pension funds became enormous capital investors beginning in the 1940s, their public sector counterparts were slower getting there. The "pension fund revolution" that Peter Drucker talked about, in which workers "owned" the US economy through their pension funds, was a fully private sector phenomenon. And yet, the "Maple revolutionaries" described by *The Economist* are all public pension funds, and together OMERS and OTPP are almost bigger than the entire private sector pension system. How do we get from Point A to Point B here?

Enter the 1986–87 Task Force on the Investment of Public Sector Pension Funds. Mandated to determine how pension investments could "best serve the pension beneficiaries and [advance] the province's economic development," the Task Force requested briefs from those they considered relevant stakeholders—unions, pension funds, financial investors, and retirees, mostly—and hosted a seminar in Niagara-on-the-Lake, Ontario, to invite discussion from experts in the pension industry. From that seminar and commissioned reports from pension experts, Chairman Malcolm Rowan submitted the Task Force's final report *In Whose Interest?* in late 1987.[32] It would fully change the shape of capitalism in Canada.

The importance of DB pension plans was taken as the Task Force's first principle; restructuring Ontario's public sector funds into DC plans was a fringe position in the pension community. James R. Fisher of Weston Foods wrote to Rowan suggesting that "money purchase [defined contribution] is the only equitable approach"—another example of the Weston family's long history of going out of its way to screw working people. But knowing the unpopularity of that notion, Rowans suggested that Fisher keep his mouth shut at the seminar in Niagara-on-the-Lake, lest he be tarred and feathered.[33]

The issue was not the structure of the plans themselves. There was little appetite for a dismantling of OMERS, the TSF, or any of the other big public sector funds. But there was a frustration that public sector pension funds were governed by a different set of rules than their private sector counterparts, rules that restricted what they could or (more importantly) *could not* invest in, rules that essentially gave government full authority on their internal governance. The problem, ultimately, was that the pension fund revolution—the transformation of workers' savings into investment funds—had not fully reached the public sector pension system, leaving billions of dollars in potential investment capital untouched. It would be the Task Force's job to open the vault.

THE MORALITY OF THE MARKET

So what did OMERS and the TSF look like in 1986? What was the problem with Ontario's public sector pensions that needed to be fixed? In 1986, OMERS had a total asset value of just under $8 billion, a near quadrupling since the beginning of the decade. Beginning in the late 1970s, it had been allowed to take on some market investments, but it still owned over $1.5 billion of Ontario government debt, bonds that the provincial Ministry of Finance required it buy at a lower interest rate than a regular private purchaser would enjoy. The TSF, meanwhile, held a $10 billion port-folio that was restricted to solely government bonds bought at below-market rate, placing an artificial cap on how much the fund could potentially bring in in returns.[34] The rate of return on the government bonds held by OMERS and TSF was a major point of irritation—they received a lower rate than a regular investor would, meaning that functionally the government was borrowing from its pension funds on the cheap. And, more importantly, neither was fulfilling its full potential as massive capital investment pools, which would be achieved through the full investment of its assets into the private market.

For workers, marketization—investing pension contri-butions in private capital markets—represented a pathway to a potentially higher rate of return and therefore a pot-entially more secure pension. OMERS's rapid growth since its conversion into a market fund showed other funds what they were potentially missing in terms of market returns. Whereas the Treasurer's office determined the interest rate at which the provincial government borrowed from its pen-sion funds, and thus put artificial caps on fund revenue in exchange for the security of a guaranteed return (whereas there are no guarantees in equity markets), the higher risk of market investments opened up the possibilities of far greater returns.[35]

While the labour push for marketization was in this way largely pragmatic, the government's eagerness to reform was laden with ideology, fuelled by cries of "won't somebody please think of the taxpayer!" For Premier David Peterson, this was a long-time hobby horse. As an MPP in the late 1970s, he had vocally complained in the Legislature about how his own position as a taxpayer left him on the hook for the welfare of a "privileged group of people"—old-age pensioners, famously an extremely privileged demographic—in the event that the TSF had a funding gap that would have to be filled by government cash injections.[36] Once in the premier's office, shifting the "burden" of public sector pensions away from the taxpayer and onto the market was a significant priority.

The Task Force agreed with the government, saying in its report that "the taxpayer's interest [was] not adequately taken into account in a number of public sector pension funds" and that both the TSF and OMERS could be restructured so as to better "represent" the taxpayer's interest.[37] "The government," they wrote, "has a fiduciary responsibility to the taxpayer to act like an employer when it is the employer."[38] In this context, "acting like an employer" meant investing the pension fund in the private market, and the notion of a "public" was substituted for the taxpayer, a citizenship role replaced by a fiscal one. Inflected with the antitax language of the New Right, Ontario politics realigned around an understanding of the "taxpayer" rather than the "citizen," forging an antigovernment politics around the taxpayer as a moral figure.

For finance, meanwhile, tens of billions of dollars in capital entering private markets was an appetizing prospect. In the wider context of deindustrial capital flight, Richard Deaton suggests, the private and public pension systems were identified by manufacturer's associations and chambers of commerce as a potential source of dynamism that could stave off economic stagnation—a political position we hear echoes of today.[39] Marketizing the TSF, then, was a move with wide consensus across stakeholders. No longer would below-rate government bonds place a ceiling on the potential rate of return for pensioners, no longer would the taxpayer be liable for any funding shortfalls, and no longer would capital markets lose out on tens of billions of dollars in investments.

This shift would not simply represent a change in pension finance, it would overhaul the Ontario government's entire financial outlook. State access to credit plays a determinant role in economic development, and the public sector pension funds were a primary source of credit. Given that cities and provinces rely on bonds to finance infrastructure expansion, pension funds for public sector workers took on a vital role as financiers. This was not just an Ontario phenomenon—the ebbs and flows of pension money had tremendous implications for municipal governments and the urban-level welfare states they supported. Indeed, the climax of the mid-century "urban crisis" in the United States—New York's bankruptcy near-miss in 1975–76—hinged heavily on pension funds as state bondholders, with municipal employees' pension funds functionally bailing out their own employer.[40]

By the mid-1980s, almost half of Ontario's total debt was owned by pension funds at below-market rates—with almost a quarter held by the TSF alone.[41] The pension funds were their main creditor, and government programs fully relied on that borrowing. In a political climate in which government borrowing was increasingly seen as contra to notions of fiscal responsibility, it was unacceptable that the state should be able to borrow for cheap from workers' pension savings. Similar pearl-clutching about morality, thrift, and hard work that had been historically used to support the employer-based pension model were thus mobilized to support marketization. Financial industry representatives, in their briefs to the Task Force, suggested that government borrowing from the large pension funds left them "insufficiently disciplined" by market forces.[42] And organized labour was just as distrustful of the state as it was of finance. In their brief to the Task Force, the Ontario Federation of Labour (OFL) complained of workers' pensions acting as a "captive source of cheap capital" for the provincial government, with no input from workers themselves.[43]

The marketization of pension funds would be more than just a monumental shift in pension policy—it would be a dramatic change in how the entire state operated. A few years earlier, the 1981–82 Royal Commission on Pensions had suggested that "the time [had] come for a radical change in the investment of assets in public sector pension plans. The financial implications for provincial finance *may be disconcerting initially*, but the results will be beneficial in the long run."[44] No longer would the Ontario government have access to a "captive source of capital" to achieve its political ends; instead, they would have to borrow at market rates. Such a change would encourage increased fiscal discipline and discourage borrowing, a necessity for neoliberal policymakers looking to strip back the Ontario state. The Government of Ontario "making itself poor" through pension reform will go on to play an important role in this story.

Pension reform would therefore serve the dual purpose of boosting capital markets *and* keeping the government in line. As the Pension Investment Association of Canada put it, "capital flows can be redirected out of the public sector back into the private sector" while "forcing government into the market will encourage more productive uses of acquired funds."[45] Government spending would be more responsible if borrowing was more expensive and if bondholders could punish government for perceived frivolity. This was placed in contrast with a potential scenario in which government controlled pension investments and used them to pursue economic development ends via the state. "There have been suggestions," wrote Malcolm Rowan to Ontario Chief Economist Bryne Purchase, "that pension investments could reflect more directly the government's economic priorities. A contrary argument is that public capital markets are reasonably efficient in the allocation of capital and are therefore the best route to economic enhancement."[46]

The question of market vs. nonmarket investments, then, was ultimately a bigger question about the correct avenue for economic development. Should economic policy be set by the invisible hand or by government? In their recommendations, the Task Force chose the former. "As a matter of principle," wrote Rowan in the Task Force's Recommendations, "public sector pension funds should invest only in market investments."[47] Marketizing pensions, then, was ultimately an ideological determination that the market was superior to the state, not just for the financing of retirement but also for economic development. That government had easy access to credit for social policy *and* that welfare was derived from nonprofit ends were simultaneously unacceptable to the wider pension community. More money in capital markets? Good! Lower cost to taxpayer? Good! Privatized economic policy? Great!

IN WHOSE INTEREST?; OR UNDER WHOSE CONTROL?

The title of the Task Force's final report, *In Whose Interest?*, reveals its major concern. The answer to the question "for whom are pension funds invested?" would, in their eyes, determine who should ultimately control investment policy and towards what ends. With billions of dollars at play, this was and is a high stakes question. And, given that the Task Force had already determined that the market is better than the state when it comes to economic development, the next question was who would wield the power to direct investment into the market. The construction of a legal scaffolding to protect pension fund investment from the meddling fingers of trade unions and the government was a central concern of the 1986–87 Task Force, who via their determination of "in whose interest" would by extension determine both who would control pension investments *and* to what ends.

Labour control over massive pension funds has always been a spectre haunting both capital and policymakers. The fear of pension funds enabling large-scale social investment was not a new one: American conservatives in the 1930s were worried that the Social Security Trust Fund could be used to build public housing, hospitals, and schools.[48] The World Bank emphasized in the early 1990s that publicly operated funds could be forced to invest in such things as public housing and therefore steps should be taken to ensure their operation within private markets.[49] If pension funds were to have enormous sums of capital at their disposal to invest, care had to be taken to ensure they could not be instrumentalized to challenge the market. Pension investments should reinforce the status quo, not challenge it.

The Task Force thus was a battleground between labour and the dual alliance of finance and the state over who would control pension investment policy. This battle was pitched early on—in October 1986, multiple labour leaders wrote an angry letter lambasting the government for underrepresenting labour in the commission. "The Task Force," they wrote, "has been directed to consult with the bureaucracy and the financial community to the exclusion of the plan participants and the unions which represent them."[50] Finance was being prioritized over labour, and they were not happy about it.

Looking through the Task Force's archive, it was clear to me that the unions were right to be frustrated. A who's who of bankers, financiers, and industrialists gathered at meetings to share their interests as the Task Force prepared to make the necessary changes for the day's "economic and financial environment" and determine the "impact of this new capital on financial markets." Presentations to and consultations with the "financial community" were the main priority for Malcolm Rowan and company as they put together their final report.[51] Meetings with trade unionists, meanwhile, appeared to be something of an afterthought. "In Whose Interest?" appeared a rhetorical question—the pension fund members themselves seemed to be pretty low priority.

But labour's concern was not only that the Task Force was being undertaken entirely in finance's interests—they were also scared of the government using their pension money for its own political goals. In their joint letter to Premier Peterson, multiple union presidents reaffirmed that "the primary purpose of the investment of the assets of public sector pension plans must be to achieve the best returns within the bounds of prudent financial management."[52] On this issue, ideological divisions within the labour movement, which carry to this day, were already beginning to manifest. Teachers took the hardest line against investment strategies based in anything other than rate of return, with Doug McAndless of the Ontario Teacher's Federation (OTF) writing his own, separate, letter to Peterson taking "strong exception to the suggestion that public sector pension plans can be 'creatively used' . . . for social development."[53]

Though all the unions were concerned about the government's political usage of pension capital, the question of the pension funds and their role in "economic enhancement" is one that segments of organized labour took seriously then and continue to now. Peter Drucker's provocative (and incorrect) suggestion that socialism had

come to America in the form of pension fund equity holdings kickstarted a series of speculative attempts to theor-
ize *how* pension investments could potentially be wielded
towards transformative political ends.[54]

Labour thought that maybe, *just maybe*, their pension
funds could save North America from deindustrialization
and help produce something vaguely resembling a just
society.[55] In 1978, American economists Jeremy Rifkin and
Randy Barber published *The North Will Rise Again,* a tract
that called for state governments and pension funds in the
American Midwest to come together to reindustrialize the
Rust Belt through the creation of public- and community-
owned firms.[56] Through the 1980s and 1990s, some private
sector unions responded to deindustrialization by using
their pensions to take over factories that would otherwise
be closing due to capital flight.[57] In 1983, the Federation
des Traveilleurs du Quebec set up the Solidarity Fund as
essentially the "best case scenario" of workers' capital—a
retirement savings fund run entirely by trade unionists and
not mandated to maximize profit.[58] Reflecting their dimin-
ishing ability to shape capitalism through collective action,
labour unions in the US and Canada sought to instead
become participants in it through their pensions. As will be
discussed more later, though, turning workers into capitalists does little to reform capitalism.

In other places, governments had explicitly identified
public sector pensions as a key instrument for economic
development. During the Quiet Revolution, Quebec con-
solidated its public sector pensions into the Caisse de
Depot at Placement du Quebec ("the Caisse"), designed
to link Quebecois' retirement savings to national economic
development through a left economic nationalism. For
those pension reformists in Ontario who were a little less
married to neoclassical economics, the Caisse offered an

intriguing model as to how pension investments could be directed towards the ends of direct economic development. Indeed, the Task Force invited Jacques Parizeau, the former Quebec finance minister, to present at the Niagara-on-the-Lake seminar—he declined, citing a prior engagement—and they also asked the Pension Investment Association of Canada whether they should merge all of Ontario's public sector pensions into a Caisse-size megafund so as to be a "player on the global market."[59]

The prospect of an Ontario "Caisse"—which would have been an enormous beast of a fund, combining the TSF, OMERS, and other major funds such as the Healthcare of Ontario Pension Plan—was an undesirable one for multiple constituencies. The final report said that "all who commented on this issue" opposed consolidating other large public sector funds into OMERS and transforming it into a megafund like the Caisse.[60] They had been warned by the "financial community" that, were the TSF and OMERS to be merged, the fund would be so big as to potentially have an outsized impact on Canadian capital markets, and that financial institutions would be better equipped to "meet the global challenge" through private sector deregulation rather than through public sector centralization.[61] Concerns were also voiced that a centralized public sector pension fund would be increasingly vulnerable to political interference, thereby undermining the private sector's right to determine economic development. Advised that OMERS itself was opposed to such a merger, municipalities across Ontario all wrote to Rowan sharing their council motions opposing the consolidation of the public sector funds.[62] Ultimately, the Task Force determined that Ontario's public sector pensions were already sufficiently centralized, thereby assuaging fears of that much capital flooding Canadian markets.[63]

The question did not fully die until a few years later, however. In the early 1990s, the Ontario New Democratic Party (NDP) government briefly floated a merger of the public sector pension funds as a potential way of managing both the short term problem of economic recession and the longer term problem of deindustrialization. The province's conservative press, however, already engaged in a propaganda war against the "scary socialists," attacked the plan as a pernicious scheme to use workers' retirement savings to fund a radical political agenda.[64]

Hesitancies over the political ramifications of government control of that much capital dovetailed with frustrations from workers that they lacked control over their own retirement savings. Public sector unions were adamantly opposed to an Ontario Caisse as well.[65] Jeanne Wellhauser's complaint of government paternalism was backed by CUPE Ontario and the OFL, who opposed state control of pension investment for the same reason private sector workers had opposed employer control of their pension funds. Echoing Wellhauser's letter, Roy Schotland— Georgetown law professor and keynote speaker at the Niagara seminar—lambasted the condescension of existing pension governance policy:

> Whether or not employees share control, it is wrong to have exclusive employer trustees . . . it is simple hypocrisy to say that the pensions are run for the benefit of mature, competent adults but they cannot have a voice, and an ear, in decisions about how the plan is run.[66]

These concerns over the paternalism of the pension system are a perfect example of how marketizing processes were seen as potentially liberating, a way of escaping the heavy hand of the state. Ironically, embedding public sector plans in the market was seen by organized labour not just as a pathway to greater rates of return, but also potentially to increased political control. Marketization would resolve the problem of government paternalism, if workers were able to exercise control over investment strategy.

The Task Force's final report explicitly conflated marketization and emancipation, counterposing a "more market-oriented approach" with the preexisting "paternalistic" one.[67] But liberation from government control created a new sort of paternalism, replacing the heavy hand of the Treasurer's office with the opaque control of investment professionals. While organized labour had hoped that marketizing pensions would mean control over investment policy, the Task Force thought otherwise. Even though the teachers unions fully agreed with the Task Force that their entire pension fund should be invested in private markets, the Task Force took care to note to the Treasury that "how TSF assets are invested is not a teacher decision."[68] The marketization of the teachers' pension would occur because government wanted it to, not because teachers were demanding it.

But the spectre of labour control, given aspirations towards social investment, was a frightening one. Indeed, there were fears that, given the amount of capital in play, organized labour could use pension funds to establish a "parallel political system" to the state.[69] The Task Force assumed that full labour control was part of CUPE, the Ontario Public Service Employees Union (OPSEU) and the OFL's "real agenda" in pursuing public pension reform.[70] The desire for union control and political investment criteria was rooted in a vision that economic policy should be worker-driven and that pension funds should not be making investments antithetical to their own members' interests. As the Canadian Labour Congress's Bob Baldwin put it at the Niagara seminar, members' interests "[go] beyond investment risk and return" when social factors and job security enter the fray.[71]

But interests beyond rate of return were seen by the Task Force as a violation of two key concepts in pension law, both of which were accepted as fundamental during the 1980s Ontario pension reforms: the prudent man principle and fiduciary duty. The prudent man principle and fiduciary duty establish that a pension fund's internal governance structures must prioritize care and caution in investment decisions. A pension fund is governed by trustees, whose legal obligation is to "prudently" manage the money held in trust—the retirement contributions of its members—this is the trustee's "fiduciary duty." Making investment choices with an eye towards anything other than prudent management is a violation of this sacred tenet of pension fund governance.

"Accepting unionization, South Africa, environmental policies"—all of these were identified by Malcolm Rowan as potential interests that unions might want to pursue through their pension investments. Labour's desire for economic democracy was driving a move to gain control of the pension funds.[72] And pension activism was already occurring, much to the Task Force's chagrin. As part of the wider push to boycott the apartheid regime, Ontario nurses had pushed their pension plan to divest its holdings in South African gold mines, a movement about which Rowan had expressed concerns. Were the government to prohibit South African investments via legislation, its compliance with the prudent man principle would be "debatable." But his fears ultimately ran far deeper than simply prudence. Give an inch to labour when they demand a shift in investment strategy and they would take a mile, he worried.[73] The echoes of this are felt today in the battle for Israeli divestment, as pension funds and other financiers fall back on the insistence that their sole responsibility is rate of return to escape scrutiny for their investment in apartheid.

The Task Force eventually resolved the question of "in whose interest" by determining that "he who bears the risk should decide."[74] Given that DB plans saw the employer assume more risk as part of the "pension deal," it naturally followed that the employer should have a certain degree of control over plan governance. But more was required to ensure that pension funds were singularly focused on the issue of rate of return—it was not enough to assign investment decision-making to financiers. There needed to be legal architecture that would guarantee that investment performance would be the sole consideration. To ensure this, then, the Task Force doubled down on the principles of fiduciary duty and the prudent person, codifying that investment performance be the sole factor to be taken into consideration when investment professionals—not labour, not the government—were making choices about how to invest public sector pensions.[75]

For finance, government, and labour, marketizing public sector pensions represented their emancipation from the paternalistic control of the state. But that did not mean that control would be socialized. The sacrosanct principle of the prudent person, coupled with the embedding of pensions in the market, simultaneously kneecapped labour plans for economic development and a significant government source of financing. Pension funds were capital investors now, independently operated, and for the sole purpose of achieving returns on contributions.

To acknowledge labour's (really quite reasonable) claim that it was unjustifiable that they be locked out of any control over their own pension funds, the Task Force proposed governance reforms that would give the major constituent trade unions a certain degree of control over the internal operations of the plans while creating labyrinthine systems of legal regulation and technocratic governance infrastructures to insulate the funds from democratic control. "Defending capitalism from democracy," through policies such as these pension reforms, has been a key component of the neoliberal political project.[76]

OMERS and OTPP are both designed as jointly trusteed plans, with a 50/50 division of control between labour and employer representatives. Both, however, have internal infrastructures designed to minimize the power of labour's hypothetical 50 percent control. OMERS's governance is divided between two corporations—the Sponsor Corporation and the Administration Corporation. The structure of the pension plan—benefit and contribution rates, primarily—is in the hands of the Sponsor Corporation. Control over investment, however, is legally consigned to the Administration Corporation, which has broad independence to exercise what it deems to be fiduciary responsibility to ensure the plan's long-term economic viability. The plan's various investment arms are controlled under the umbrella of the Administration Corporation, siloed off from the limited democratic control of the Sponsor Corporation.[77] Although labour has half of the board seats on the Administration Corporation, requirements related to technical expertise and a background in finance limit how much power can actually be wielded there. The board at OTPP is similarly encased from democratic control—while 50/50 between the government and the Ontario Teachers Federation (OTF), intense requirements related to professional experience and knowledge in the accounting and investment worlds again circumscribe any opportunities for real rank-and-file input.

The governance of OMERS and OTPP was carefully designed to keep investment decision-making in the hands of financial managers and hired professionals, ensuring that workers' retirement savings would be instrumentalized to reinforce the market and not for any other purpose. But it should also be mentioned that most unions who have voices on these boards are okay with this dynamic. Recall the letter the president of the OTF wrote to the Task Force, insisting that no considerations other than rate of return should be contemplated when making investment decisions. Labour does not speak with a unified voice in these boardrooms, in part due to differences in philosophy surrounding the structure of the system itself. While some, such as the nurses pushing for divestment from South Africa, see their pension investments as a reflection of their bigger political priorities, others choose to focus in on what is best for their pensions. And often, groups try to choose both. Such is the nature of a system laden with insurmountable contradictions.

THE GLOBAL MAKING OF THE "CANADIAN MODEL"

The restructuring of OMERS and the OTPP into investment funds took place within a wider global context of pension reform beginning in the 1980s, in which the role of state-supported retirement was looked on by policymakers and financiers with increasing scrutiny and the private market with greater zeal. Pension marketization in Ontario occurred alongside a worldwide shift in pension policy to the right.

Pensions occupy a unique and important place in the global history of neoliberalism. In Chile, the transformation of the state pension system into a universal defined contribution scheme was a major policy undertaken as part of the neoliberalization project of Augusto Pinochet. In 1981, the Pinochet regime, guided by a University of Chicago–educated finance minister, used the newly individualized private pension system to flood the country's stock market with investment capital, setting up the "Chilean example" for other countries to follow.[78]

And follow it they did. Looking towards public pension systems in the Global South and the former Eastern Bloc as a potential gold mine for private capital, the World Bank helped lead a concentrated ideological push by neoliberal intellectuals and institutions to transform the financial basis for retirement worldwide. By 2004, thirty countries, predominantly in Latin America and post-Communist Europe, had privatized their pension systems in some way or another, whether through the replacement of state schemes with individual retirement accounts or the creation of mandatory or optional private schemes to supplement pay-as-you-go state models.[79]

In 1993, twenty-five years before they were celebrating the successes of the "Canadian model," the World Bank published an influential report on global pension restructuring. *Averting the Old Age Crisis: Policies to Protect the Old and Promote Growth* forwarded the neoliberal institution's proposed revamping of pension systems worldwide. Its aim, perhaps most succinctly articulated by its subtitle, was to encourage reforms that would prioritize the reduction of public pension provision and shift emphasis towards a system based on private funds integrated into capital markets, which would have the dual effect of financing retirement and bolstering accumulation processes.[80] The specific policy recommendations differed based on a country's level of development, but the overarching theme was that pensions should be in service of markets, whether that be through privatization or financialization.

In the liberal welfare states of the Anglosphere, this attack on pensions manifested as an onslaught against the state-managed contributory schemes. Embedded within welfare systems that already had a significant role for the market (as showcased through the employer-based pension system), the growing financial strain of the public pension system represented a problem for governments with an ideological inclination towards market solutions.[81] As "social security reform" became the dominant issue of the day in the United States and United Kingdom, the Canadian federal government under Jean Chretien sought to overhaul the CPP as part of a wider domestic antiwelfare politics that sought to reduce state obligations for social insurance. While the right-wing Reform Party pushed to replicate the Chilean model of mandatory individual retirement accounts, a consensus quickly emerged between the Liberal federal government and Conservative provincial counterparts that marketization, rather than privatization, of the CPP was the preferable option.[82] In late 1997, the federal government established the Canada Pension Plan Investment Board (or "CPP Investments") to act as the private investor for the public contributions to the CPP.

The establishment of CPP Investments as a result of federal-provincial negotiations solidified the transformation of Canada's public pension scheme into a market actor that would quickly grow to be far and away Canada's largest pension fund, dwarfing the Caisse, OMERS, the OTPP, and other major ones. Even a country like Canada, which avoided the privatization-frenzy that consumed Latin America and Eastern Europe, was swept up in the neoliberal pension-financialization-mania as it turned the state pay-as-you-go scheme into one of the world's largest institutional investors, capstoning the pension reform the Task Force on Investment of Public Sector Pension Funds had kickstarted with a final grand marketization of the public pension system.

Nevertheless, even amid a global individualization of retirement—demonstrated both through privatization and through the rise of DC schemes—Canada has retained a central role for a public pension in the state welfare sector and DB schemes in the employer-based public sector. Indeed, salvaging DB plans was and continues to be a policy priority for the Ontario government. To the chagrin of some in the pension community, the 2007 Ontario Expert Commission on Pensions was explicitly tasked with ensuring the actuarial health and safety of the province's remaining DB plans and encouraging their expansion rather than exploring any possibility of DC-ization.[83] All this was occurring as conservative provincial finance ministers in Alberta and British Columbia—jumping on the 2008 financial crisis—floated the idea of mandatory provincial DC plans to supplement (rather than replace) the CPP.[84]

But Ontario's massive DB funds survived and thrived in private markets, as did CPP Investments. The global spirit of pension marketization filtered into Canada through the reforming of the OTPP in the 1980s and the CPP in the 1990s, producing the massive capital funds that were able to take on cost-intense investments in real estate and infrastructure. Though the "Canadian model" of pension funds was developed through domestic reforms—the so-called Maple Revolution—it was nevertheless the product of a worldwide shift in how states approached retirement in the age of the Washington Consensus *and*, as we will find, a shift in how real estate related to global finance in the age of deindustrialization.

CONCLUSION

On New Years' Day 1990, the capstone was placed on Ontario's pension reform by the official conversion of the Teachers Superannuation Fund into the Ontario Teachers' Pension Plan, a market-investing public sector pension fund that would operate by the same rules regarding investment and governance as any private sector fund.[85] The pension fund revolution had officially come to Ontario's public sector.

"Do you, sitting at the center of this action," wrote Georgetown Professor and Niagara seminar keynote speaker Roy Schotland to Malcolm Rowan a week after the seminar's conclusion, "have the sense I got of being 'present at the creation . . .' of modern pension law in Canada?"[86] The marketization of the TSF and its conversion into the OTPP fundamentally changed the landscape of both retirement and capitalism in Canada. Public sector pensions in Ontario had by the 1990s been pushed into the ocean of private capital investment, part of a global re-entrenchment of capital's domination of social welfare systems. As deindustrialization gutted private sector unions and their pensions, policymakers, public sector unions, and the financial community all coalesced behind plans to withdraw pensions from government debt and invest them in capital markets like their private sector counterparts.

For labour, this was as much part of a push for control over investment policy as it was a push for higher rates of return. For policymakers, it was an effort to reduce the state's responsibility for social welfare. And for finance, it was intended to apply the discipline of the market to both pensions and government, opening new lucrative avenues for investors. As Keith Ambachtsheer, an extremely influential Canadian pension investment consultant, put it in his newsletter: "These [were] exciting prospects for Canadian investment professionals!!!"[87]

The end result of this process of marketization was the development of the OTPP and OMERS into crucial institutional investors at the same time as the political economy of Canada shifted away from industry and towards finance and real estate. That same political-economic shift coincided with a shift in the centre of gravity of Canada's labour movement, away from the private sector towards the public, and a shift in the politics of social reproduction towards a deepening reliance on the market. It is to the history of that new working class, welfare, and the urban landscape that we now turn.

TWO

Pensions, Property, and Poverty

In 1995, five years after the establishment of the Ontario Teachers' Pension Plan (OTPP), Ontario elected the Progressive Conservative Party led by Mike Harris. Campaigning on a platform of neoliberal policies called the "Common Sense Revolution," Harris and his party sought to totally reshape Ontario's politics through a war on the social state and a realignment towards capital. Attacks on public sector workers and the welfare state had been key parts of Ontario's politics since the 1980s but were accelerated by the Harris government through the 1990s and early 2000s. Meanwhile, the private welfare of those same workers was being used to undermine the security of everyday life for the broader working class in Ontario and worldwide.

These changes in work and welfare were felt on the urban scale. The downloading of welfare expenses onto municipalities collided with the wider implementation of austerity-minded urban governance regimes to restructure how social reproduction in the city was organized, both in terms of its labour and its provisioning. The financialization of necessities like real estate intersected with the implementation of workfare programs and cutting of social security in Ontario at the turn of the millennium.

Meanwhile, the newly marketized Ontario pension funds started building big portfolios in real estate and infrastructure. As capital realigned away from the real economy and towards rentier capitalism, OMERS and OTPP helped lead the charge. Urban restructuring—which privatized infrastructure, opened floodgates to real estate speculation, and screwed the working classes (including the members of the plans themselves!)—produced ample opportunities for Ontario's pension funds to grow from their small potato origins in the late 1980s to the mega behemoths that we live with today.

David Harvey describes the city as the "locus of accumulated contradictions," simultaneously the spatial expression of the dominant mode of production and the landscape upon which the revolutionary movements required to overturn it can be formed.[1] This chapter presents the history of one such contradiction. A new labour movement in the public sector was forged through conflict while their retirement savings increasingly hinged upon investment in that same conflict. Workers' pension funds grew larger and larger; housing prices rose higher and higher; surviving got harder and harder.

REVANCHIST TORONTO

Like all neoliberal cities, Toronto is a city that hates the poor. This hatred has only become more visceral and more pronounced in recent decades. Geographer Neil Smith wrote in the 1990s of the "revanchist city," an urban form in which capital—which had in the postwar period fled downtown cores and inner cities—"returned with a vengeance" by hyperinvesting in urban real estate, jacking rents and property values, and waging protracted war against those who had made their homes in the working-class city—women, people of colour, and the poor.[2] A political shift to the right in Ontario and beyond saw Toronto become a global epicentre of urban revanchism, inflected with a vicious anti-working-class politics that wedded its targeting of public sector workers to a wider politics that sought to make everyday life more expensive and more market-oriented.

Mike Harris did not invent antipoor politics in Ontario. Social democrat NDP Premier Bob Rae, by the early 1990s, was already embracing the new antiwelfare hegemony of the Reagan revolution and the Third Way. "Welfare isn't working," suggested Rae as he slashed the budget of the Ministry of Community and Social Services in 1993. Echoing the mantras of personal responsibility that had earlier on inflected pension policy, he insisted that welfare recipients show "the willingness to work."[3] Rae's shift to the right on welfare was mirrored by an attempt to "extract $2 billion from the incomes of public sector workers" via his "Social Contract," which froze public sector wages under the pretext of fiscal crisis. As the treasurer of CUPE Local 79, the Toronto municipal workers' union, put it, "The legacy of the Rae government has been to irretrievably weaken trade union rights in this province."[4]

But if a Social Democrat was rehashing the talking points of the Poor Laws, then things were going to get a hell of a lot worse with a dyed-blue Tory back in office in 1995. Wielding the vicious right-wing playbook of the "Common Sense Revolution," Mike Harris waged war on Ontario's poor until the early 2000s. Revanchism was the Common Sense Revolution's whole raison d'etre. In a series of "frontal attacks" on the poor, the left, and the labour movement, the Tory government spent its first term rolling out a whole set of market-friendly and antiworker social policies.[5] Among these were

› a 21 percent cut in welfare benefits;[6]
› a ban on "aggressive panhandling";[7]

> a freeze on new government-assisted housing;[8]
> the downloading of responsibility for social housing onto municipalities;[9]
> a reduction in local governments through amalgamations;[10]
> a reintroduction of scabbing;[11]
> a revocation of employment equity legislation.[12]

Attacks on welfare infrastructure had an intensely gendered dynamic. Cuts to welfare transfers were predicated on the assumption that unpaid women's work in the home would act as a "shock absorption mechanism" on the worst impacts of cuts, with household labour making up shortfalls left by reduced social services.[13] This, of course, did not end up being the case. Instead, women struggled to feed their families as reductions in benefits put downward pressure on household income.[14]

Cuts to education and attempts to contract-out work in the public sector catalyzed women-led strikes by both teachers and public servants through the late 1990s, linking labour conflict to a wider social movement-driven resistance to the war on welfare.[15] The OTF and OPSEU strikes worked in solidarity with the Days of Action led by the OFL to push back against the Conservative social and labour policy.[16] Community and labour came together in a spirit of "social solidarity" to protest attacks on education, healthcare, childcare, and the wider public service.[17] Attacks on public sector workers and on the poor were part of the same ideological project and were therefore opposed in tandem with one another.

These attacks on welfare and public sector work were part of a coordinated political strategy linking together governments at the federal, provincial, and local levels. The federal government passed the buck to the province, and the province followed suit by passing it to the cities. On January 1, 1998, the provincial government amalgamated Toronto with its suburbs into a megacity, which was meant to enable this downloading of welfare costs onto the municipality and, by extension, onto individuals. Rescaling put both urban public sector workers and the wider working class under immense pressure when it came to access to welfare.

The Common Sense Revolution was part of a global attack on urban welfare systems. In Rudy Giuliani's New York, for instance, the former heart of the New Deal became a laboratory for experiments in workfare policies that would reshape the city as a site for social service provision.[18] In Toronto, prior efforts in revolutionizing welfare provision through a childcare program smacked up against restructuring and rescaling to fizzle out. The downloading of welfare costs, along with the sudden changes to city governance, undermined Toronto's efforts at social welfare.[19]

The attack on social housing by the Harris government, meanwhile, put the final nail into a coffin that had been built one plank at a time over the previous two decades. Public housing starts had been in long decline since their peak in the 1970s.[20] Federal cooperative housing was cancelled in 1992 and social housing downloaded to provincial governments in 1993.[21] The Harris government's freezing, therefore, was more of a Pruitt-Igoe moment—a symbolic end of the public housing era that had already functionally ended—than a dramatic policy shift. But that long-term decline, kickstarted by changes in federal government policy in the 1970s and 1980s, had fundamentally changed the landscape of housing in Toronto and cities across Canada.

This dismantling and downloading of state welfare systems produced a phenomenon that had never really existed in Toronto before: homelessness. While precarious housing had always been endemic in the city, it was not until the social policy changes of the 1980s that thousands of people slept on the street nightly.[22] This urban class war was most definitely not taken lying down. The 1990s saw a remarkable upsurge in poor peoples' organizing, with left-wing social movements such as the Ontario Coalition Against Poverty waging ambitious collective actions in protest of the vindictive policies that both the provincial and municipal governments had undertaken in their war on the poor.[23]

The revanchist city and the real estate city are two sides of the same coin—real estate requires a vicious and vindictive war on the poor to maximize property values, and, by extension, its ability to extract rent from the land. Toronto has been transformed into a "competitive city," where labour costs must be kept low and public projects are designed to attract capital investment.[24] The demands of real estate capital play a vital role in the form of urban governance, which has taken root in Toronto. As Harvey outlines, since the 1980s there has been a broad shift in urban governance "from managerialism to entrepreneurialism," a shift from municipal governments that seek to balance the imperatives of social service provision with the needs of capital towards those that can best attract investment in the form of development.[25]

Notions of competitiveness, which drive a pro–real estate "growth machine" politics, dovetail with the desire on the part of municipal and provincial governments to discipline public sector labour through the slashing of government spending. What geographer Jamie Peck calls "austerity urbanism" has become a leading form of urban governance across the Global North, with policymakers using economic crises to institute forms of "extreme economy" that download the costs of reproduction onto the individual and engage in revanchist labour policy against the public sector.[26] Cities become the target of neoliberal reform because they are the home of the welfare state's primary constituents—the working poor and municipal unions. Indeed, austerity urbanism has particularly targeted municipal workers, as the city—led at that point by a social democrat mayor—showed in its response to the 2009 Toronto municipal strike.[27]

Austerity urbanism uses discourses of "urban crisis" to justify cutting everything down to the bone, selling everything that is not nailed down and attacking its service workers. Indeed, Mike Harris's minister of education John Snobelen said the quiet part loud in 1995 when he suggested that the provincial government should "create a crisis" in the education system so as to justify spending cuts and attacks on the OTF.[28] The slashing of budgets, downloading of welfare costs, and attacks on public sector workers all came together through the Common Sense Revolution's urban project.[29]

The needs of real estate capital were front and centre to the austerity urbanism and revanchist social policy of the Common Sense Revolution. Capital's "return to the city" goes hand in hand with the wider war against public sector workers and the poor waged by the entrepreneurial city.[30] Revanchist social policy sets the groundwork upon which real estate developers can exploit scarcity to extract huge amounts of wealth from the built environment. The time-period in which the neoliberal state has been laying out its austerity urbanist policies, thus, has been one of considerable accumulation for real estate capitalists, and, as we will get to, for the pension funds among them.

The continuous escalation of housing costs has turned Toronto into a city deeply polarized by class and race. In 2010, housing expert David Hulchanski published an

influential report on the "three cities within Toronto"—
the cities of the rich, the poor, and the middle. Since the
1970s, Hulchanski outlines, the middle-income bracket
in Toronto has cratered, with the city increasingly divided
into a rich core along the Bloor-Yonge subway line and
a working poor periphery.[31] Coinciding with the frontal
assault on labour and welfare, rent and housing prices have
skyrocketed out of control over the course of decades. The
result of escalating housing costs in Toronto has been a
crisis of the household, with debt stratification also divid-
ing Toronto along class lines.[32]

According to the Canadian Mortgage and Housing
Corporation (CMHC), an average two-bedroom apartment in Toronto costs $2120, far out of reach for many
working people.[33] Indeed, if housing "affordability" is to
be defined as one-third of income, someone would have
to make over $45 an hour in Toronto to afford a two-
bedroom apartment, almost triple the minimum wage. The
city's downtown core and suburbs have become epicentres
of gentrification and unaffordability.

And this process has been far from limited to Toronto.
Skyrocketing rents are a generalized phenomenon across
all of Ontario. A two-bedroom apartment in Hamilton is
$1762, in Kitchener, $1820. The average new house price
in all of Ontario passed $1,000,000 in 2022. The province's
urban working class has been under the gun—attacked by
welfare cuts, attacked by layoffs and union-busting, and
attacked by hyperescalating housing costs. So now we ask:
What role are their retirement savings playing in this?

THE RISE OF REAL ESTATE

We know how OMERS and the OTPP became major institutional investors. Through the late 1980s pension reform,
they were pushed two-handed into the ocean of private

capital markets. The next question, then, is how they went from being funds worth ~$10 billion to having real estate and infrastructure portfolios that are so much larger now than their entire fund value was in the not-so-distant past. The answer is that financial capital started gobbling up the urban landscape, providing the opportunity for large-scale institutional investors to make killings on land and housing.

The particularities of real estate as an investment make it very appealing to a large pension fund. As Harvey outlines, real estate is in many ways a "not ordinary" commodity. Its lack of portability and long lifespan (relative to, say, a car) lends itself to committed, long-term investment as land and improvements are fixed in space. The duration of ownership is generally long, while the moment of exchange is instantaneous, which means that large amounts of initial capital outlay are required. And, crucially, land and shelter are commodities that no one can do without, producing monopoly rights for those who own it and limiting the leverage of those who do not.[34] All these come together to make real estate a commodity that requires significant amounts of both capital and time, and large pension funds have both in spades.

Harvey's analysis is backed up by pension industry explanations as to the appeal of real estate as an investment class. "Bigger = better" for pension funds when it comes to investment diversity—the larger a fund, the more resources it has at its disposal to deal in assets that require a more particular investment skillset than simple stocks do.[35] The initial capital outlay required to develop or buy real estate, moreover, favours those funds that have billions of dollars to play with. For smaller funds, real estate and infrastructure are "prohibitively expensive" investments for direct ownership—they can only indirectly invest via large asset managers.[36] Public sector pensions, because they have so many beneficiaries, fit the mark nicely. And, crucially, the long-term horizons of a pension fund gel neatly with the profile of real estate as a commodity. A pension fund needs to have a reliable source of income so as to be able to comfortably pay out benefits over the course of long periods of time. In a public policy structure in which the continued appreciation of real estate values is taken as a social good in and of itself, a pension fund can look to real estate as a reliable source of both long-term rents and upward valuation. For the bigger plans like OMERS and OTPP, then, real estate was a deeply attractive investment. They had the resources necessary to diversify into alternatives because the economic winds were blowing towards financialized real estate.

The restructuring of public sector pension funds coincided with a shift in how real estate functioned in its relationship to massive investors and finance. The flight of capital from industrial production in Ontario and other places in the Global North catalyzed a shift in finance towards the housing economy as a source of accumulation. As Alan Walks and Dylan Simone say, "It is the lack of local profit-making alternatives in the *productive* sphere which compels private firms to shift to rent-generation, asset-value appreciation, lending, and accumulation-by-dispossession as business strategies."[37] The same can be said for institutional investors such as pension funds. Changing geographies of production shifted the primary form of accumulation for investors onto the circuit of fictitious capital, where the long-term horizons of rent and value appreciation—best seized on through real estate ownership—offered better opportunities for accumulation. For capital, the profitability crisis of deindustrialization was solved through real estate development and investment. Uncompetitive domestic manufacturing pushes capital towards real estate, from what political economists call the "primary circuit" to the "secondary circuit."[38]

As part of the Task Force's recommendations, they put together a draft list of regulations governing the investment of public sector pension funds. Beyond the initial affirmation that the "prudent person" approach should be prioritized over any secondary political aims, they also suggested particular limitations on fund exposure so as to ensure long-term security and stability. Among these suggestions was a limitation on exposure to alternatives (nonequity) investments, particularly real estate and infrastructure.[39]

The OMERS board reacted to this suggestion with shock and horror. By 1987, they were beginning to dip their toes into the water of real estate and were already pushing up against the proposed 5 percent cap.[40] "Arbitrary quantitative standards" on investment, OMERS suggested, would in fact *limit* their capacity to be prudent because a prudent investment approach required heavy investment in alternatives.[41] As early as 1982, pension investment specialist Keith Ambachtsheer (close advisor to the 1986–87 Task Force) had recommended that large funds put 25 percent of their investments into real estate.[42] Compared to this, the notion that funds should be limited to just 5 percent seemed altogether ludicrous, an arbitrary cap that would prevent the big public sector plans from pursuing an attractive alternative investment. As a result, the Task Force relented on these recommendations, leaving investment type largely unregulated.

As global economic development moved towards real estate, so too did pension capital. And real estate is a *global* commodity. In 1993, the World Bank published a policy paper, *Housing: Enabling Markets to Work*, pushing for state withdrawal from housing provision and calling for a full embedding of housing into market systems.[43] The report advanced policies that would give housing a vital role in economic development via an emphasis upon its role as an asset that could be integrated into financial systems and generate value for private owners.[44] Market hegemony over global housing systems was official economic policy. Indeed, the 1987 Ontario pension reforms coincided with the establishment of the Basel I financial accords, which established mortgage-backed securities as a AAA valued asset, incentivizing a deeper integration of real estate with the financial sector.[45]

The first phase of Ontario's pension reform and its intersection with the rise of the real estate economy hit its apex in 2000. In late 1999, OMERS moved to purchase the Royal Bank of Canada's entire real estate portfolio in a joint venture with Toronto real estate developer Oxford Properties in order to meet its target of 10–15 percent real estate exposure.[46] By the next year, it had fully bought out Oxford Properties.[47] The OTPP, meanwhile, rung in the new millennium with the purchase of Cadillac Fairview, which owned largely commercial, not residential, real estate, adding 102 buildings to their real estate portfolio in one fell swoop.[48] But it is interconnected with the wider systems of land economics that drive housing crises, even though OTPP is the landlord of very few people. It is all part of the same rancid system of financialization.

As *Benefits Canada* put it following the OTPP's purchase, "Ontario teachers are now some of the biggest players in real estate in North America."[49] In contrast with the Task Force's suggestion that 5 percent be the cap for real estate, pension plans were now searching for up to 15 percent exposure. The 2000s began with OMERS and the OTPP reaffirming their commitment to the global real estate economy through the acquisition of subsidiary corporations to manage their growing portfolios. Fifteen years prior, they had not even been fully marketized. But by the turn of the millennium, they were knees deep in private real estate.

WORKERS' REITS

Through the next few years, Ontario's pension plans kept on chugging, expanding their portfolios. But then, crisis. The 2007–08 financial crisis hit pension funds extremely hard. OMERS contracted by 15.8 percent; the OTPP by 18 percent. Revealing of the scale of the catastrophe, the cover page of the OTPP's 2008 annual report reads, "Let us explain how the economic crisis has affected your pension plan's performance."[50] Beyond the big public sector funds, the economic crash catalyzed a wider crisis of retirement when both DB and DC plans with high exposure to equity markets felt the sink intimately.[51] The debate over which is better, DBs or DCs, was renewed as DC plans collapsed and DB plans faced solvency issues.[52] Pension experts were left scrambling for solutions as the economic crisis became a retirement crisis.

The crash, however, had little negative impact on pension fund investments in real estate. As figure 2.1 shows, the small dip in Canadian pension real estate investment in 2008–09 quickly gave way to a massive and essentially consistent surge, far greater than any previous increase. Intuitively, this seems very strange. The financial crisis was, by and large, the result of a collapse in the real estate market and was intimately experienced as a *housing* crisis first and foremost by the hundreds of thousands who were foreclosed upon in the immediate aftermath of the crash.[53] To go full throttle into real estate in that context seems altogether backwards.

But capitalism is seldom logical. Indeed, when contrasted with volatile public equity, real estate was seen as

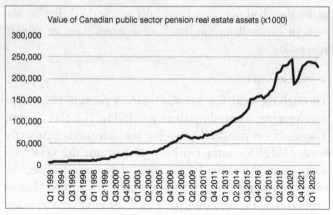

Value of Canadian pension fund assets in real estate (x 1,000,000). Source: Statistics Canada, "Trusteed Pension Funds, Value of Assets by Sector, Quarterly" (Government of Canada), accessed August 1, 2024, statcan.gc.ca.

a source of stability after the financial crash. As a 2010 *Benefits Canada* article put it, "There's security in bricks and mortar."[54] Although the crash had been caused by real estate, it had been felt directly by pension funds in their equity investments, both public and private. To investors, the "road to recovery" would be shaped by the minimization of risk. Minimizing risk meant reducing equity exposure, and reducing equity exposure meant increasing investments in alternatives. Increasing investments in alternatives meant sinking a lot of cash into real estate and infrastructure.[55] As one pension investment specialist put it in 2015, "Real estate is no longer an alternative asset. It's very well established as a core asset class for pension funds."[56]

This is because public and private equities were where the hit was felt, not real estate. When determining the reduction of risk and "downside protection," pension investors saw that Canadian direct-owned real estate

weathered the storm of 2007–08 while equities plum-
meted.[57] Even public equity real estate investment through
real estate investment trusts (REITs—a form of investment
fund in which the fund builds a real estate portfolio and
investors buy shares in the portfolio, enabling them to
invest in the real estate market without actually having to
buy properties themselves) remained appealing to pension
investors. By fall 2009, REIT boosters were suggesting in
Benefits Canada that "public market real estate companies [were] in a unique position to lead future recovery"
from the financial crisis, and encouraged pension funds
to increase their exposure to them.[58] REITs, though more
volatile than direct ownership, enable a higher degree of
liquidity for investors, allowing them to get out quick
if need be.[59] But, for the bigger funds like OMERS and
the OTPP, direct ownership remains the chiefly attractive form of investment because of reliable long-term cash
flow. As long as a building remains fully leased, it will
continue to pay out in the form of rent, providing stable
and predictable returns in contrast with the volatility of
stock markets.[60] And so, despite the fact that real estate
induced the financial crisis, it was nevertheless crucial to
how pension funds emerged from it.

This was helped along by a decade of hyperlow interest rates that fuelled the fire, allowing major asset portfolios to be built with cheap debt. This real estate-driven
economic "recovery" was aided and abetted by Canadian
public policy in the aftermath of 2007–08. The funnelling
of huge amounts of money through the CMHC essentially
re-inflated Canada's housing market, functionally bailing
out the banks even as Canada formally avoided a bank
bailout.[61] Since the crash, Canadian housing prices have
increased at a remarkable rate, producing a veritable crisis
for those not already on the property ladder.

Going hand in hand with gung-ho CMHC policy was a new and unique opportunity for Ontario's pension funds to intervene in the housing market in a whole new way— mortgage insurance. AIG's Canadian arm went under in 2009, offering the OTPP the chance to sink their teeth deeper into housing finance.[62] Coating their acquisition in nationalist language, the OTPP reorganized AIG Canada as Canada Guaranty and explicitly foregrounded the fact that it was Canada's only wholly domestically owned private mortgage insurer (as well as being its largest).[63] Through mortgage insurance, the OTPP hoped to grease the wheels of private homeownership, allowing for a continuous inflation of the Canadian housing market.

This has reverberations for retirements beyond just those of the OTPP's beneficiaries. In the absence of a robust public retirement system, the ownership of property has become increasingly vital to the financing of retirement, while the financialized asset-based welfare system has opened up new opportunities for pension funds to capitalize on the lack of a welfare state. Adding to this is the fact that pension funds are the leading buyer of CMHC mortgage bonds, which produce another link between retirement policies and the continuing upward valuation of real estate.[64]

Recently, the OTPP expanded its financial portfolio through the acquisition of HomeEquity Bank, a Canadian reverse mortgage provider.[65] This investment is particularly sinister. Reverse mortgages are used to provide senior citizens with the ability to extract equity from their property value, giving them an additional income source in old age. With housing a vital component of the neoliberal asset-based welfare model, reverse mortgages offer a source of income for those without access to a good solid pension.

In truly perverse fashion, then, a retirement savings fund capitalizes on and directly exploits the *absence* of a robust retirement system by loaning money against older peoples' houses. Keeanga Yamhatta-Taylor writes of what she labels "predatory inclusion," wherein access to capitalism can be just as exploitative as exclusion.[66] The practices of private real estate finance—whether they be renting, mortgage insurance, or reverse mortgages—prey upon those in desperate need of both safe shelter and money to finance retirement. Increased access to household debt means increased exposure to the predations of finance capital, and, in this case, the exploitations of the pension fund.[67]

The promotion of homeownership is central to the neoliberal welfare system in which owning a house and building wealth is designed to be a substitute for a real pension system, which places retirement security in tension with increasing housing unaffordability.[68] The overall aim is to have workers be literally invested in the system such that their own economic stability relies upon wider market stability. This dynamic structures asset-based welfare, in which continuously rising housing prices are taken as an automatic social good because of their role in wealth accumulation, and the pension fund, in which retirement rests upon financial returns.[69] This is a system in which finance is protected while the individual absorbs the risk. CMHC and Canada Guaranty mortgage insurance protects lenders, while borrowers—who depend on asset access to finance their retirements—are left to the wolves. Collective responsibility for social security has been replaced by the organized redistribution of risk and responsibility onto atomized individuals via individual asset ownership and the taking on of huge amounts of debt. Meanwhile, the only form of collectivized retirement security remaining—the public sector pension—actively makes things harder for those who have been pushed into the abyss of a fully individualized retirement.

In a deeper irony and contradiction, the labour relations regime that has emerged to roll out neoliberal capitalism—an economic system in which public sector pension funds play a crucial role—has also targeted those same public sector pensions. Despite pension funds being crucial to the accumulation system, they also represent to capital a form of public sector bloat, a luxurious privilege held by greedy public sector workers that the wider state can ill-afford. Thus, simultaneously, neoliberalism needs public sector pensions while also attempting to destroy them, like a snake eating its own tail. Hundreds of thousands of individual DC accounts could not play the same vital role in capital accumulation as a single DB plan, and yet capital attempts to cannibalize them nonetheless. The neoliberal desire to download risk to the individual comes into conflict with the needs of capital accumulation. But, as we have seen, sometimes marketization is more useful to capital than privatization and, thus, the public sector funds survive.

PENSION FUND CITIES

Real estate is a global commodity and so pension capital links Canadian workers to urban landscapes *worldwide*, connecting local gentrifications in other countries to Ontario's particular public sector labour context. Pension capital flows in and out of global cities, creating a network of interconnected built environments. Cadillac Fairview's and Oxford Properties' portfolios expanded globally through the 2000s. It would be easy for me to simply catalogue the respective portfolios of Cadillac and Oxford, but I would rather provide here a broad sketch of a few choice investments that illuminate the scale on which they are operating.

Cadillac Fairview and Oxford Properties have significant local portfolios in Toronto, in both residential and commercial real estate. Oxford-owned residential towers are scattered across the Greater Toronto Area, from the heart of the financial district to the suburbs of Brampton and Mississauga.[70] They share a landscape with over twenty Oxford-owned office buildings across the metropolitan region. Sprinkled alongside them are Cadillac Fairview's shopping malls and skyscrapers, which similarly structure Toronto's vertical geography.[71] Both Cadillac Fairview's and Oxford's portfolios, moreover, have presences across Canada. Canadian real estate has been a lucrative investment in recent years as housing prices have grown increasingly unaffordable.

Canadian pension fund landlords, meanwhile, have been among Canada's worst evictors. A 2020 investigation by *Briarpatch Magazine* found that major Canadian pension funds are heavily invested in REITs with nefarious track records of evictions and rent increases.[72] The *Toronto Star*, meanwhile, exposed that PSP Investments—the pension fund of the federal public service—was entering a $700 million partnership with US company Pretium, a fund that had exploited the foreclosure crisis to dramatically expand its portfolio after 2008.[73] PSP Investments has come under consistent fire on this issue. The fund has a joint portfolio with real estate company Starlight Investments, which has been the target of a protracted rent strike in Toronto since mid-2023. PSP's and Starlight's efforts to raise rent above Ontario's rent control pushed tenants to begin withholding rent, which the pension fund responded to with eviction filings.[74]

Pension capital also flows across oceans. London, England, has become a city by and for the 1 percent, and investments in its real estate by Oxford Properties have contributed to its continued status as a hub in the global real estate economy.[75] In 2013, Oxford went in on a joint venture with Crown Estate, the real estate arm of the British royal family, to redevelop St. James's Market in the London downtown, a project with a final price tag of $400 million. The project's aim, an Oxford representative suggested, was to "transform" a historic corner of London in collaboration with monarchic wealth.[76] This followed on the heels of their first investment in the British capital, which came in 2010 through their acquisition of Watermark Place on the Lower Thames.[77] Luxury London is a pension fund landscape.

This brings us back to Hudson Yards, where we began. A monument to private capital accumulation, Hudson Yards is the largest private real estate development in American history. Hudson Yards development was a top priority during the mayoralty of Michael Bloomberg, who ushered in a particular ideological paradigm of neoliberal urbanism rooted in a valourization of technocratic management and fetishization of luxury.[78] The "Bloomberg Way," as geographer Julian Brash calls it, was the culmination of the processes set into motion by the city's fiscal crisis in the 1970s, the ultimate affirmation of finance's and real estate's hegemony over development politics in the city.[79] His own personal identity as the ultimate manager, along with the specific orientation of his City Hall towards real estate development, emphasizes New York's role as the greatest symbol of neoliberal urbanism.

The development of Hudson Yards was a vital component of this process. As early as the 1990s, real estate developers looked at the west side railyards with dollar signs in their eyes. During the Bloomberg administration, his economic development team—led by Deputy Mayor Dan Doctoroff, who had previously spearheaded a plan to make Hudson Yards development the epicentre of a New York Olympics proposal—devoted significant attention to transforming the west side railyards into a new neighbourhood for luxury commercial real estate.[80] The eventual Hudson Yards plan, initiated in the aftermath of the 2008 financial crisis, saw $25 billion sunk into the built environment to build sixteen structures, including five thousand apartment units and five commercial office buildings.[81] Beyond simply being a building development, the Hudson Yards scheme consciously forwarded itself as a process of spatial production, in which the ambitious investment of Oxford and Related Companies would transform Manhattan's west side.

Although much of the equity came from the project's two primary developers—Oxford and Related Companies—the neighbourhood development project on the west side of midtown was the beneficiary of, according to a report from *Gothamist*, approximately US$5.6 billion in public money, whether in tax breaks or direct payments.[82] Investigative reporting from Kriston Capps of *CityLab*, moreover, showed that US$1.2 billion of financing for the project came via a subsidy program designed to encourage real estate investment in economically deprived areas. "Creative financial gerrymandering," as Capps phrases it, resulted in luxury Hudson Yards being placed in the same "urban distressed area" as five large public housing projects in Harlem, over four miles away from the development site.[83] The Hudson Yards megadevelopment—a luxury project on an unprecedented scale—used money intended for Harlem to finance the construction of the crown jewel of the real estate state.

Oxford Properties and Cadillac Fairview have reshaped urban environments worldwide through their real estate developments, using public money and subsidies to build "landscapes of power" representing the conquest of the city by capital. Canadian workers' retirements hinge upon gentrification and wealth extraction, the result of an economic system that views peoples' homes as assets to be managed rather than as places to live.

CONCLUSION

In January 2022, Oxford Properties sold a skyscraper it co-owned in Toronto's financial district. The Royal Bank Plaza, jointly owned by the Ontario Municipal Employees Retirement System and CPP Investments was sold to a Spanish investor for $1.2 billion. If the monumentality of Hudson Yards represents financialized real estate at its peak, then the Royal Bank Plaza's *ancien regime* decadence illustrates luxury real estate's absolute contempt for the poor. Why? Because the building's façade is literally lined with gold.[84]

Ontario is ground zero in a global housing crisis, its municipal workers the target of austerity, and their pensions deeply invested in financialized real estate. All three of these processes unfolded simultaneously and continue to structure urban capitalism, not just in Toronto but in cities worldwide—regardless of whether or not they are financial centres. Cadillac Fairview and Oxford Properties, though they are headquartered in Toronto, have a global footprint, the product of a real estate economy that defies borders and in which Canadian pension funds play a critical role.

Though direct investments in luxury developments jump off the page as obvious examples of pension interest in the real estate economy, recent years have seen an expanded pension fund involvement in more subtle elements of real estate finance. Investments in REITs, mortgage insurance, and, most recently, reverse mortgages show how the totalizing grip of finance over the housing economy has, indeed, implicated pension funds.

A war on welfare and on public sector work unfolded simultaneously as part of a broader onslaught on social reproduction in Ontario. But this onslaught coincided with the increasing investment of public sector workers' welfare in that same attack. There are a lot of moving parts to keep track of here. Pension marketization was part of a wider welfare restructuring but also accelerated that restructuring through investment strategies. Public sector workers were on the receiving end of austerity while also having their retirements linked to the accumulation engine governing that austerity regime. The housing system was increasingly financialized while those pensions, which are ultimately meant to pay for things like housing, deepened their reliance upon that same financialization. The contradictions mount!

What are the political options, then, for a union movement that should be fighting for a broad sense of workers' rights in the city but has its hands tied by its retirement savings? To that question, we will return.

THREE

Local Labour, Global Infrastructure

"So here you have at Yonge and Finch, the Ontario Teachers' Pension Plan, but [the global] is the scale that we're operating on. We're swapping an airport on one continent for two airports on another."[1] Referring, in 2011, to a deal in which the OTPP traded an ownership stake in Sydney Airport in Australia for ownership positions in airports in Copenhagen and Brussels, Ontario Teachers' Pension Plan (OTPP) CEO Jim Leech summed up with remarkable casualness the scale and nature of Canadian pension fund investment. Airports are items to be swapped around like baseball cards, profitable trinkets in the global trading game. Gas pipeline networks in the United Kingdom, Italy, and the United Arab Emirates all share a common investor—the OTPP.[2] And what do Indian toll roads, Nova Scotian public schools, Chilean natural gas facilities, and the Port of Melbourne have in common? They are all owned by the Ontario Municipal Employees Retirement System (OMERS), financing the retirement of Ontario's municipal workers.[3]

Infrastructure is everything. At risk of sounding cliché, it is society's skeleton, all the physical formations necessary to make the world function. But also, perhaps more crucially, infrastructure is the base of political economy. Commodity circulation—from point of production to consumption—is entirely reliant on infrastructure. Capitalism lives and dies with the quality of its highways and port facilities. And the reproduction of the worker is an infrastructural process, facilitated by hospitals and schools, water pipes and transit systems. You could not have a medieval economy without infrastructure, and you sure as hell cannot have a twenty-first century one without it.

Beyond just enabling profitability under capitalism, however, infrastructure is itself a source of enormous potential wealth. The ownership of critical infrastructures allows monopoly rights and accompanying rents to all those who rely on it. It is for this reason that infrastructure privatization has become such a critical component of postindustrial rentier capitalism.

The privatization of key infrastructures is the latest chapter in capitalism's *longue durée* process of enclosure. Taking everything once held in common into private ownership saps away at the last vestiges of the social state and allows for the extension of profit-making into areas it had not previously reached. Capitalism puts up fences around all it can find, seeking profit opportunities wherever possible. And when productivity has been sapped everywhere else, profit must be found in the nooks and crannies of everyday life. As Brett Christophers aptly puts it, "Our lives [are] in their portfolios."[4]

Canadian pension funds developed much of their fame in the investment world off their infrastructure portfolios. They were at the cutting edge of the rise in alternative assets, especially as few pension funds invested directly in infrastructure—choosing to instead work through intermediary asset managers. The portfolios of the big Canadian funds are jaw-dropping—their reach is wide and deep, penetrating almost every aspect of everyday life in most corners of the world.

For decades, Canadian unions (and Canadian Tories!) panicked about the political implications of American ownership of Canadian infrastructure. It is ironic, then, that Canadian pension funds—not just any Canadian investor, but one in which the labour movement has such a stake—would have become among the biggest players in the global trade of infrastructure assets. For all that activists were worried about foreign ownership in Canada, OMERS and OTPP are now among *the biggest foreign owners* of infrastructure worldwide.

Canadian pension funds have been key players in the global enclosure of the commons, as critical infrastructures have fallen into private ownership and been the means through which enormous amounts of wealth have been redistributed upwards. This chapter outlines how Ontario's pension funds have sunk their teeth into infrastructure as an asset class, taking advantage of the neoliberal turn to enmesh themselves into the fabric of society.

PUBLIC PENSIONS, PUBLIC UTILITIES, PRIVATE OWNERSHIP

The financialization of OMERS and the Teachers' Superannuation Fund (TSF) represented a wholesale shift in the politics of infrastructure. While pensions had previously been crucial to state infrastructure development via the purchasing of below-market government bonds, they now play a vital role in developing infrastructure through private means.

Governments used to build things! It is almost unthinkable now, but it used to happen. The building of the postwar welfare state was to a large degree (although not so large in Canada as in the European states where the built environment had to be essentially rebuilt following World

War II) an exercise in infrastructure development. These infrastructure buildouts were financed by bond sales, and—as discussed in chapter 1—the public sector pension funds were far and away the largest holders of those bonds. Ontario built infrastructure directly, but it was financed indirectly by the pension funds that were a significant source of state finance. By cutting off one of its primary sources of funding, the Ontario government suddenly put itself in the position to be cash starved. Alongside the growing power of finance capital, the foundations were set for a new period of infrastructure development in which private finance and private ownership replaced public spending.

And as infrastructure became a game for private investors instead of government, both OTPP and OMERS built *massive* portfolios. Teachers' infrastructure holdings, at year-end 2022, totalled $39.8 billion, with an additional $10 billion in natural resources. Together, they formed the fund's third biggest asset class, behind only private equity and bonds. For OMERS, the portfolio is slightly smaller ($26.8 billion in infrastructure), but that made it the fund's second biggest asset class, only trailing public stocks. Real estate and infrastructure still get called "alternative assets," but that name has become something of a misnomer. They have entered the core for the big funds.

The infrastructures that have been targeted by pension funds as lucrative investment opportunities, Heather Whiteside suggests, are also those that are "too socially integral to fail."[5] Twenty-first century society cannot exist without hospitals and highways, without schools and sewage systems. That integrity is what gives the pension funds surety of returns. And in political contexts where governments face infrastructure deficits and are manically obsessed with getting "shovels in the ground," it gives them breadth of options.

And so, the "socially integral" section of the big fund portfolios has grown steadily over the last years. OMERS especially has been eager to build out its portfolio in Ontario's healthcare system. The fund got heavily involved in public-private-partnership (P3) projects put forward by the provincial government to "fix" its infrastructure gap—by 2019 it owned three hospitals and twelve nursing homes, all of which it neatly packaged into one bundle to sell to another asset manager.[6] Until summer 2024, the fund also owned LifeLabs, the largest medical laboratory company in Canada.

This is because when pension investment professionals look at population demographics, investments in healthcare and eldercare infrastructure become extremely appetizing, even though their beneficiaries are the same people who get screwed over when those infrastructures get privatized. In 2017, a *Benefits Canada* article outlined how healthcare infrastructure represented a serious "growth opportunity" because of changing demographics. Their sentiment was clearly shared by the pension fund industry. CPP Investments owns a 15 percent stake in a French long-term care company, Orpea; PSP Investments owns Revera, a company that, until 2023, held a huge portfolio of retirement and long-term care homes in Ontario (it still owns them but no longer manages them, having repositioned towards treating the facilities as investment properties); and OTPP owns Amica, a chain of luxury retirement homes in BC and Ontario. Pension funds have looked at population demographics with dollars signs in their eyes and have financed the exploitation of the elderly.[7]

The P3 model of infrastructure development, emerging from an era in which governments "made themselves poor" through tax cuts and pension reform, has produced terrible infrastructure. Ontario's love affair with P3s has been (and still is) torrid and passionate and has produced nothing but disasters. Toronto's P3 transit expansions have been an unmitigated disaster, governed by the strange public-private entity of Metrolinx and laden with a never-ceasing pileup of construction delays, while Ottawa's P3 transit expansions resulted in an LRT that stops working if someone coughs in its general vicinity. An emphasis on P3 development has meant that Ontario still does not have enough hospital beds or nursing homes and does have highways that are falling apart.

Unions have consistently opposed P3s as part of a bigger, pro-public service vision, but advocates of P3s have used pension fund involvement as a legitimating excuse to attempt to override that opposition. A 2017 report by Paul W. Bennett of the Atlantic Institute of Market Studies suggested that Nova Scotian public sector unions should support the private ownership of school facilities because the beneficiaries, ultimately, would be Ontario municipal workers.[8]

Indeed, the undeniable power of Canada's pension funds has been even more recently used as government's justification for doubling down on P3s. Faced with domestic infrastructure deficits, both federal and provincial governments have attempted to persuade those pension funds that between them manage assets close to Canada's GDP to reorient towards Canada. The 2023 Fall Economic Statement from Finance Minister Chrystia Freeland included multiple references to a desire to onshore more Canadian pension capital. Potential structural policy changes meant to encourage domestic investment—a removal of a cap that limits pension funds to a 30 percent equity share in most Canadian companies chief among them—were coupled with broad, vibes-based suggestions that the federal government could persuade the big funds to pivot back towards the home market.[9] Coming out of the Fall Economic Statement, the federal government announced in its 2024 budget the formation of a "working group" led by the former president of the Bank of Canada to develop legislation that will encourage domestic pension fund investments.

A few weeks earlier, the Government of Ontario announced the creation of a provincial Infrastructure Bank to streamline the delivery of private capital to infrastructure projects. Its messaging at every stage has foregrounded the importance of the big Ontario-based pension funds. As the announcement's foreword put it, "Having institutional investor support will help the government build more infrastructure, while creating opportunities for Canadian pension funds to put their members' investments to work right here at home."[10] This is economic nationalism for the neoliberal age. Investment capital will be onshored, returned from the foreign lands where it has been planted, to make sure that it is used "right here at home."

Other commentators have identified pension fund investments as a potential solution to structural problems in the Canadian economy. Responding to the suggestion that Canada has a "productivity problem," influential members of the financial sector (along with the former chief economist of the Canadian Auto Workers) wrote an open letter calling for Canadian pension funds to increase domestic investments to spark economic growth.[11] Although pension funds have been among the main drivers of the rentier economy, they are suddenly being identified as the solution to rentierism's built-in precariousness.

For what it is worth, the response of the pension funds themselves has been slightly more tepid. The OTPP's statement on the announcement of the Infrastructure Bank, released the next day, was short and sweet:

> As a pension plan providing retirement security for
> 336,000 working and retired teachers in Ontario, we
> invest in global markets to provide the diversification
> and long-term performance to ensure that the plan
> remains fully funded. We welcome opportunities to
> add to our $25 billion investment portfolio in Ontario
> and look forward to engaging with the government to
> learn more about new projects created by the Ontario
> Infrastructure Bank.[12]

The explicit justification of OTPP's primarily global
investment portfolio reads as a subtle rejoinder of the
"invest Ontario pensions in Ontario" undercurrent of
the government's announcement, while myriad distancing
verbs—"welcoming opportunities," "look[ing] forward,"
"learn[ing] more"—indicates a degree of hesitation.
For OTPP, Ontario is small potatoes: if the investment
is right, they will do it, but there is no grand provincial
romance to it.

The federal government's comments on public sector funds, meanwhile, catalyzed an even more tren-
chant response from the CEO of the Alberta Investment
Management Corporation, who took to the pages of the
Globe and Mail to lambaste the finance minister's attempts
to "interfere" with the Canadian model's widely heralded
"stand-alone pension investment firms with unambiguous
missions" and "strong, independent governance." To him,
the *new pension nationalism* (my words, not his) threat-
ens the very core of the pension reforms discussed in the
first two chapters of this book. The 1987–88 Ontario
Commission and the 1990s CPP reforms were based on an
adamant assertion that government needed to stay out of
the pension funds—suddenly interventionism is re-entering
the picture, albeit in totally different ways.

The CEO's suggestion to the feds, if they really wanted more domestic pension fund investment, was more infrastructure privatization. "Making large-scale infrastructure projects currently owned by the Government of Canada available for private investment," he wrote, "would be another useful demonstration of Ottawa's desire to increase pension-fund investments in Canada."[13] One is left wondering how privatizing already-existing infrastructure would help the policy goal of building new infrastructure, but it is revealing of the investors' state of mind. The federal government, for its part, has heeded the advice and announced intentions to open Canadian airports to private investment, potentially appetizing for those funds that had so gregariously bought and traded European airports throughout the 2010s.

All in all, the pension industry's reaction to government outreach reveals its steadfast commitment to the basic premise of the entire system: rate of return is all that matters and social impact and policy goals should be kept out of the pension system. But despite the tepidness, the Ontario government's description of the "win-win-win" nature of pension fund infrastructural investment—government gets investor support, workers get pensions, society gets infrastructure—parrots the public relations strategies of the funds themselves. In 2021, OMERS commissioned social impact studies from the Canadian Centre for Economic Analysis, looking to quantify their contribution to Ontario society. Needless to say, when the narrow prism of econometric analysis is used to quantify OMERS's "positive impact," the conclusions are very different than those of the book you are currently reading. Measured monetarily, the impact of OMERS is immense: $11.9 billion in GDP, split nearly 50/50 between the circulation of pension payments and the reverberations of investments.[14]

In a sense, though, the report elegantly reaffirms one of the central points of this book: Ontario's pension funds are fully sewn into the economic fabric of the province.

Of additional interest is that OMERS's own summary of the reports drew specific attention to the plan's relation to healthcare employment—one in fifty-four healthcare jobs is "supported" by an OMERS investment.[15] In a province in which the piecemeal privatization of the healthcare sector is a pressing and credible threat, such a statistic about the relationship between health employment and private capital produces more concern than solace. It is also striking given that healthcare workers—especially paramedics—form a significant component of OMERS's membership. A system in which OMERS helps privatize Ontario's healthcare system is one in which the fund is an architect of its own destruction—because private sector workers struggle for pension access more so than their public sector counterparts.

The Ontario Infrastructure Bank, the government has noted, is especially meant to build out the province's social infrastructure, with an emphasis on long-term care homes, energy, and transportation. Pensions already own large parts of Ontario's social fabric, and the hope is that they can end up with more of it.

All of this is not to say that pension investment in infrastructure is, in and of itself, negative. The P3 structure ensures that pension fund ownership produces mediocre infrastructure to the detriment of wider society, but this need not necessarily be the relationship pensions have to infrastructure projects. The answer is not simply that we should nationalize all the infrastructure. As left critics of nationalization observe, public ownership and worker ownership are not the same thing. Prefinancialization pension economics show that neatly—the labyrinthine networks of state finance meant that workers' savings were being used for government projects without mechanisms of democratic control, let alone democratic ownership. Ontario's expansionist modern state of the 1960s and 1970s, though it was underwritten by pension money, offered little space for those pension's beneficiaries to drive policy.

But while pension funds financing public infrastructure through bond purchasing allowed for governments to simply draw upon captive pension capital to pursue their own particular economic development strategies, a more activist form of bond purchasing could dovetail nicely with a wider campaign on labour's part to renew domestic infrastructure and reinvest in the physical sinews of a just society.

Could an infrastructure bank be a modernized—dare I say, democratized?—form of the prefinancialization pension structure? The major funds could fund it, much like they had previously bought huge amounts of Ontario Treasuries, but with higher amounts of direct input on allocation and strategy. Instead of a return on investment based on expectations of profit—as in the P3 structure—return could come through the prevailing coupon rate. Pension fund capital could be a source of leverage in endeavours to expand social infrastructure, but through the public sector.

This absolutely does not solve the pension contradiction, but it is a potential stopgap. Right now, pension fund financing means privatized infrastructure. It means hospitals, schools, airports, port facilities—the physical backbone of society—being milked for rents and those rents then going back into the pockets of the workers who themselves rely on the infrastructure. Society crumbles to finance the retirements of those who will pay the price for society crumbling. It is all out of whack. And it is not limited to Canada.

PENSION GEOGRAPHIES

The tentacles of the Canadian pension fund are far reaching. It is reflective of a totally bananas system that the largest real estate project in US history and some rural public schools on the Canadian East Coast are owned by the same entity—and reflective of an *even more bananas* system that that entity is a pension fund. And yet, that has become a remarkably normal state of affairs.

Travel the world with Canadian pension funds in mind and you will find that you cannot escape them, no matter how hard you try. On a recent trip to London, everywhere I went I was greeted with the logo of Thames Water—maintenance vans, sewerhole covers, sidewalk grates. Thames Water was, frankly, inescapable. Thames Water might be, perhaps more than any other company, the best symbol of the horrors of pension fund capitalism—just as Hudson Yards is a remarkable synecdoche for the modern system of financialized real estate, so too does Thames Water encapsulate the modern system of financialized infrastructure.

Thames Water is owned by OMERS, in partnership with a few other investors, including the British Columbia public sector pension. It has been owned by this consortium since 2017, but its history of privatization goes further back than that. Margaret Thatcher's Conservative Government privatized the UK's water utilities in 1989, creating a government utility regulator—Ofwat—and clearing the debts of the preexisting utilities so that profiteers could start with a blank slate.[16]

Thames Water is an unmitigated disaster, hemorrhaging money, charging exorbitant rates, and skirting environmental regulations. In September 2023, it was fined £100 million by Ofwat for not meeting sewage spill targets for a third straight year, just months after having been fined

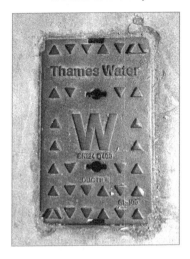

A Thames Water sewerhole cover, stumbled upon in south-east London. Photo taken by author, October 2023.

£3.3 million for a separate one-off spill.[17] All the while, the company is falling apart. In June 2023, faced with exorbitant debt levels related to infrastructure renewal (apparently the pipes are bursting!), and already having maxed out shareholder cash injections, Thames Water was forced to put out a bond issue at an enormous premium just to fulfill its basic obligations.[18] The UK government has had to draw up contingency plans for a scenario in which the company went bust, including temporary nationalization.[19] Ironically, the supposedly left-wing British Labour Party, for its part, has stated that it has no interest in renationalizing water utilities.

Revelations continued to roll out even following the levelling of fines and the debt crisis. In November 2023, *The Guardian* reported that Thames Water had dumped 72 *billion* litres of sewage into the River Thames. A Liberal Democrat MP lambasted the British government for "standing idly by whilst our rivers are poisoned and water firm execs pocket millions."[20] It is all the more embarrassing that such ecological devastation cannot be simply blamed on a single dipshit CEO but instead leaves the entire Canadian pension system red in the face. Speculation grew that, barring another major cash injection from OMERS and its partners, Thames Water could go under in April 2024 (it managed to hang on).[21] The company is also under investigation from the national water regulator over potential dividend payments to shareholders.[22]

Thames Water has become an enormous symbol in the UK of the failures of privatization. It has continuously been front-page news through 2023 and 2024, both for its backroom calamities and for its horrifying impacts on the day-to-day lives of Londoners. Reports of water-borne illness due to contamination came in May 2024, while—in a rare instance of the misfortunes of Oxford and Cambridge evoking anything other than schadenfreude—the famed Oxford-Cambridge rowing race was threatened with cancellation due to the risk of splashing water causing participant illness.[23] And now the saga has hit its climax. OMERS wrote off its investment in Thames Water in June 2024, accepting it as a dead asset on their books and as a loss that will have to be stomached going forward. The stage is now set for, likely, a renationalization of London's water infrastructure.

OMERS' ownership of Thames Water has not coated the fund in glory—indeed, it has coated the fund in sewage. The privatization of critical infrastructure has yielded nothing but misery, from ecological devastation to skyrocketing utility bills. That workers in Canada can only afford to retire because of this suffering from their British counterparts makes it an altogether terrible scheme. Fascinatingly, however, the pension angle has not been a key component of the many, many condemnations of Thames Water. The horrors of pension fund capitalism are so aggressively normal at this point that pension ownership does not even warrant a mention outside of an aside.

But Thames Water is just a single suction cup on a single tentacle of the Canadian pension octopus. If you were to take a "spot the pension fund" vacation, the odds of your flight going through a Canadian pension-owned airport are very decent—Mr. Leech's reference to "swapping airports" that opened this chapter is an apt distillation of the entire Canadian pension investment model. Across Europe especially (airports in Canada have—for now—evaded privatization, even as their governance was restructured during the 1990s privatization-mania), airport investments became a hot item for Canadian funds. Airports in London, Birmingham, and Brussels are all owned by OMERS, and more were owned by the pension funds when Leech made those remarks in 2011.

But the circulation of goods is more lucrative than the circulation of people, and so port facilities are also critical to these portfolios. Port facilities, which in many countries had historically been nationalized as critical infrastructure (in Canada they remain so), have grown into lucrative investments amid the rise of "just-in-time" supply chains. For one of the major OMERS port investments, the prehistory is similar to that of Thames Water—a Thatcherite privatization. OMERS has owned a major share in Associated British Ports, which manages a quarter of the United Kingdom's shipping trade, since 2006. The expansion of Canadian pension funds into port ownership was so vigorous that, in 2017, *Benefits Canada* called it a "love affair" and a "frenzy."[24]

Many of the key nodes of the unbelievably precarious international trade system are owned, through the pension funds, by Canadian trade unionists. Even though the pandemic turned "supply chains" into a household term, and the seemingly distant world of global shipping suddenly felt remarkably intimate, our own financial relationship to the ports never came to the foreground. But as Deborah Cowen argues, the world of logistics is the defining industry of twenty-first century capitalism.[25] To locate OMERS and OTPP within that world is to underscore that we are living in pension fund geographies.

Perhaps more significant than any other asset class, however, is energy. Almost half of OTPP's infrastructure portfolio is in energy, and OMERS has significant exposure to it as well. Many of these investments are in public power utilities, ranging from the production to transmission stages. OMERS wears its ownership of Ontario's Bruce Power—an enormous nuclear power facility that supplies 30 percent of the province's electricity—as a badge of honour, citing it in every report where it reaffirms its positive contributions to the province. In a strange ownership arrangement, meanwhile, OMERS also has a very small stake in Alectra Utilities, the otherwise entirely municipally-owned electricity utility that covers areas in the north and west of the Greater Toronto Area. OTPP, for its part, is co-owner of Enwave, a company that provides energy structures for buildings across the province.

The reach of this investment segment, however, is beyond Ontario. Pipelines in Texas form a major part of the OMERS portfolio—a $1.4 billion outlay in 2018 secured their 50 percent stake in a system linking crude oil in West Texas to refineries and shipment in Houston—while Puget Sound Energy, the primary power utility for a decent chunk of Washington State, is co-owned by OMERS and OTPP.[26] Not to be outdone on pipelines, OTPP also owns pipeline networks connecting gas fields in the United Arab Emirates to power plants.

Most corners of the world are touched, in some way

or another, by pension fund infrastructure portfolios. They cannot be escaped because they are the basis of everyday life—the water we drink, the electricity that lights our homes, the schools we attend.

WELFARE COLONIALISM AT HOME AND ABROAD

The pension fund exploitation of land and life, highlighted by all of the energy investments, has a particularly colonial tenor. The long history of settler colonialism in Canada by its nature produces a relationship between Ontario's pension funds and the multigenerational theft of land in Turtle Island, but that relationship rises to the surface when the dispossession of Indigenous Peoples forms the direct cash basis of a settler working-class retirement. That is the case for so many of the energy investments described above— the pipelines, the terminals, the utilities—but it is nowhere more unsubtle and in-your-face than in the example of Heritage Royalty, a wholly owned subsidiary of the OTPP.

Heritage Royalty, to put it simply, owns everything beneath the surface of a very large swathe of Alberta. If you are an oil or mining company drilling on their land, you are paying rent to Heritage Royalty. They are a mineral rights royalty holder. Mineral rights royalties take colonial land holdings and distill them into their purest form—sources of rent from extraction. Indeed, the "History" section of Heritage Royalty's website traces their colonial basis better than I ever could:[27]

> › 1676: King Charles II of England grants 948 million acres of fee title land to the Hudson's Bay Company. This land includes much of modern-day Alberta, Saskatchewan, and Manitoba.
> › 1868: The Hudson's Bay Company transfers the deed of title to the Dominion of Canada in exchange

for £300,000 Sterling (C$1,500,000). However, the Hudson's Bay Company retains 5 percent of its most arable land.

› 1881: The Dominion of Canada grants 25 million acres of fee title land to the Canadian Pacific Railway ("CPR") in consideration for completing the section of the transcontinental railway from Manitoba to British Columbia. CPR selects agricultural lands from the odd-numbered sections of townships in a broad belt straddling the railway's right-of-way, creating a "checkerboard" pattern of land ownership.

› 1886: CPR returns 7 million acres of fee title lands to the Dominion of Canada after completing the railway. CPR sells 5 million acres of fee title land to various land syndicates.

› 1905: The Dominion of Canada grants large, contiguous blocks of fee title acres (including mines and mineral rights) to CPR in consideration for completing irrigation projects to improve the habitability of lands in Saskatchewan and Alberta. One of the land blocks granted is the 1.8mm acre Palliser Block in southeast Alberta.

› 1912: CPR begins to reserve mines and mineral rights during land sales. CPR leases its mineral rights to companies interested in developing the minerals, and collects royalties on the subsequent production.

› 1958: CPR creates the Canadian Pacific Oil and Gas Company ("CPOG") to hold its fee title land.

› 2015: The Ontario Teachers' Pension Plan ("OTPP") acquires Cenovus' fee title and GORR lands for C$3.3 billion, creating Heritage Royalty.

Heritage Royalty's millions of acres in private mineral rights are the direct outcome of centuries of land theft by the British Crown, the Canadian state, and the railroads. If you were to try and name a Holy Trinity of colonialism in Canada, those three would be the Father, Son, and Holy Ghost. That is the history the company proudly claims, and the history that OTPP continues—drilling rights on explicitly stolen land. And although Heritage Royalty can say on its website that it is "not directly involved in any oil and gas exploration or production," and the OTPP can neglect to mention their role in oil extraction in their *Annual Responsible Investing and Climate Strategy Report*, the pension fund is very blatantly the inheritor and perpetuator of a long legacy of colonialism and environmental destruction.[28]

But to truly understand the colonial logics of the Canadian pension system requires a wider scope. Canadian pension funds have $177,481,000,000 wrapped up in infrastructure investments, as of mid-2022. Of that, $138,137,000,000 is in foreign holdings. That is 77.8 percent. Much is in the United States and Western Europe, true. But exposure to "emerging markets"—the official finance world term for the Global South—has grown significantly in recent years. Of the total OTPP portfolio, 15 percent is in Asia and Latin America, while 13 percent of OMERS is invested in Asia and "Rest of World." The aggressive unfolding of neoliberalism across the postcolonial world laid the groundwork for what are now significant opportunities for financiers in totally private infrastructure networks.

In 2016, only 6.3 percent of the OMERS portfolio was outside of Canada, the United States, and Europe.[29] And so it feels apt that Chile—ground zero of financialized pensions and the sell-off of everything but the kitchen sink—is where OMERS first invested in South America at a moment when its profile in the Global South began to grow. In

2017, they bought a significant share in GNL Quintero, a natural gas terminal that holds a monopoly on the gas sector in central Chile.[30] Energy utilities, as discussed above, are a perpetually appetizing asset. While OMERS cashed out of GNL Quintero in 2022, OTPP continues to have a decent exposure to Chilean utilities, owning shares in both electricity transmission and water there.

Within the emerging market surge, Canadian pension money has been greeted with open arms by right-wing governments across the world as part of private infrastructure development agendas. The Brazilian government of Jair Bolsonaro had a positive and productive relationship with Canada's pension funds. Upon his election in 2018, the CBC enthusiastically played up the opportunities for Canadian capital to cash in on privatization and deregulation: "Brazil's new president elect, Jair Bolsonaro, is a right-winger who leans towards more open markets. This could mean fresh opportunities for Canadian companies looking to invest in the resource-rich country."[31] Little did they know that his election would not only present grand opportunities for Canada's natural resource investor class but also for those investors who are hypothetically in the business of providing social welfare.

Following the long tenure of the social democratic governments of Lula and Dilma, Bolsonaro entered office with ambitions towards reversing their expansion of Brazil's public sector and going one step further by selling off whatever he could. By the second half of his government, with the writing on the wall about his chances in the 2022 Brazilian election, Bolsonaro identified CEDAE, the state-owned water utility for Rio de Janeiro, as a top target. Shortly before the auction, CPP Investments, alongside AIMCo, bought heavily into a Brazilian company named Igua Saneamento in order to get Igua's bid over the line.[32] For CPP, "support[ing] the privatization of water and sewage services" in Rio was an end-of-year highlight in 2022.[33]

Just as Bolsonaro's ascent to office spelled serious cash for the Canadian welfare "state," so too did the 2014 election of Hindu nationalist and economic hardliner Narendra Modi to the prime minister's chair in New Delhi. From his first days in power, Modi sent positive signals to foreign investors—Canadian pension funds chief among them—that his government would rip down barriers to their investments in the country's infrastructure stock. Within six months of his election, *Bloomberg* was already highlighting the Canada Pension Plan's eagerness to expand its nascent India portfolio.[34] Indeed, by early 2015, CPP Investments was committing to major infrastructure and real estate investments just as Modi himself was visiting Toronto on a wooing mission for Canadian finance.[35] Six months after that, CPP Investments opened an office in Mumbai, and prominent Indian government officials were proclaiming the board's interest in a $2 billion investment in the city's affordable housing stock.[36] Since those early pushes, Canadian pension fund commitment to Indian infrastructure has accelerated and deepened. In 2022, the Indian government explicitly called for Canadian pension funds to further their investments in the country's infrastructure programs.[37]

As Pranab Bardhan notes, India's significant infrastructural deficit has greatly inhibited its ability to replicate China's boom since the 1990s and has therefore become a focus for the Modi government. In Bardhan's analysis, the Indian state itself has limited capacity to take on the infrastructure projects necessary to fill this gap, and the historical experience with P3s has been laden with regulatory problems.[38] Modi's goal, made explicit to prospective

investors early on in his tenure, was to make private infrastructure in India a lot more appealing to foreign capital.

And, if Canadian pensions are anything to go by, he
succeeded. The Canadian funds—CPP Investments and
OTPP especially—have gleefully sunk their teeth into the
Indian market. An infrastructure buildout for a country of
over a billion people, financed largely by private capital?
It represents a remarkable opportunity for institutional
investors like pension funds with the pocketbooks and
long-term horizons able to commit to it. And so, the pension fund portfolios in India have grown dramatically.

OTPP's India portfolio has grown at a remarkable pace
and in areas that touch every aspect of society. In 2021
and 2022, the fund bought a significant stake in the Indian
government's Infrastructure Investment Trust, building
a portfolio of eight toll highways in some of the country's most populous states.[39] A few years earlier, OMERS
bought into a separate group of Indian toll roads.[40] In a
fact that is likely no coincidence, the OMERS fund manager who made that deal—OMERS's first entry in India—
was poached by OTPP a year later and has been at the
forefront of their escalating India focus. Underscoring how
climate politics can get caught up in webs of colonialism
and finance, another of their highlighted investments has
been designed to "capitalize on the growing renewables
opportunity" and "decarbonization ambitions" in India.[41]
Partnering with the Mahindra Group, OTPP is looking to
aggressively expand the country's renewable sector, antici-
pating major growth opportunities. OMERS has also
recently sunk its teeth into India's solar sector.[42]

These investments in India also show that the commodification of the social safety net is not just a North American
or even just a Global North phenomenon. As part of
OTPP's rapidly expanding investments in the country, they

acquired a majority stake in Sahyadri Hospitals Group, the largest private hospital chain in Maharashtra, India's second most populous province. Such an investment points towards the globalization of privatized healthcare and the role of Canadian pension capital within it. Sahyadri CEO Abdalrari Dalal happily labelled OTPP as an "ideal partner" for the company as it seeks to "take up a larger role in the healthcare delivery ecosystem" in India.[43]

In September 2022, OTPP opened an office in Mumbai to manage its new swathes of infrastructure investments. As OTPP President Jo Taylor put it, "India is an attractive investment destination and will be one of our growth markets over the next 5–10 years. It has a large, growing, and dynamic economy, with openness to foreign capital which makes it a strategically important market for us."[44]

OTPP's level of engagement with India accelerated to such an extent that its growing portfolio there warranted a special level of attention in its 2022 annual report. Highlighting a few key investments of the fund's $3 billion exposure, they also quoted their India point-man Deepak Dara as saying that the country's "openness to foreign capital and growth trends" are "aligned to our strengths."[45] When announcing the escalation of their highway investment, the plan highlighted its growing relationship with the Modi government.[46]

Given India's twentieth-century commitment to state-driven modernization, a softly socialist path guided by heterodox development economists, its commitment to a modernization scheme reliant entirely upon the private sector is a radical shift. Modi's modernization scheme—while couched in a similarly nationalist language—is based on privatization, with a minimal role for the state and with an emphasis on foreign capital that perhaps contradicts its nationalist costuming. As capital pivots from China towards other "emerging markets," the Bharatiya Janata Party has actively positioned itself as a receiver of foreign investment.

The gung-ho attitude of Canadian pension funds towards their investments in far-right privatization programs in India and Brazil is especially striking considering their willingness to toss notions of "fiduciary responsibility" aside in moments of neo-Cold War sabre rattling. In January 2023, OTPP announced the cessation of its direct investments in China, and a few months later it closed its Hong Kong office.[47] Recent tension between Canada and India, however, (in which India's commitment to domestic fascism clashed with its commitment to global capitalism) so far appears to have not impeded the alliance between Ontario's pension funds and Modi's private modernization strategy. Just as State Department operatives in the 1930s could confidently say, "He may be a son of a bitch, but he's *our* son of a bitch" about Anastasio Somoza (or about Josip Tito, or Nicolae Ceausescu, or whichever US-supported dictator you like), so too can the Canadian pension funds identify an ally in Narendra Modi and an enemy in Xi Jinping. All it took was a shot down weather balloon for the OTPP to get the hell out of dodge with regards to investment in China.

As Israel escalated its onslaught on Palestine in 2023, meanwhile, it raised war finance—$6 billion in the first month—through bond sales to "select investors" in private auctions, mediated by Goldman Sachs and the Bank of America. Selling at additional premiums, these auctions attracted many buyers who were more than willing to publicly reaffirm their pro-Israel bona fides—state governments across the United States—but even more who hoped to keep their names out of the headlines.[48] Given the international reputation of the big Canadian pension funds, it is hard to conceive of a world in which they were not asked to be among the "select investors." And we know that Canadian pensions are major investors in Israeli banks and in the weapons companies that have armed genocide in Gaza. In January 2024, organizers with Labour For Palestine outlined that major Canadian pension funds—CPP, the Caisse, PSP, OMERS, British Columbia Investments, and OTPP—collectively had $1.6 billion invested in the major arms companies that supply the Israeli military.[49] BDS activists, meanwhile, have revealed that CPP Investments owns upwards of $16 billion in companies that actively participate in either the genocide or in the illegal settling of parts of occupied Palestine.[50] Activist teachers who are members of OTPP have also drawn attention to their pension's investments in major arms companies that support genocide in Gaza.[51] Canada's relentless support for Israel is appalling enough—it is additionally horrifying that our welfare systems are used to enable colonial genocide.

Welfare state structures in the imperial core, it has to be said, have always been reliant upon colonial plunder—even if that plunder now takes a different form. As Kwame Nkrumah, the first prime minister and president of independent Ghana, wrote in his classic *Neo-colonialism: The Last Stage of Imperialism*:

> The problem which faced the wealthy nations of the world at the end of the second world war was the impossibility of returning to the pre-war situation in which there was a great gulf between the few rich and the many poor. Irrespective of what particular political party was in power, the internal pressures in the rich countries of the world were such that no postwar capitalist country could survive unless it became a "Welfare State." There might be differences in degree in the extent

of the social benefits given to the industrial and agricultural workers, but what was everywhere impossible was
a return to the mass unemployment and to the low level
of living of the pre-war years.

From the end of the nineteenth century onwards,
colonies had been regarded as a source of wealth which
could be used to mitigate the class conflicts in the capitalist States and, as will be explained later, this policy
had some success. But it failed in its ultimate object
because the pre-war capitalist States were so organized
internally that the bulk of the profit made from colonial
possessions found its way into the pockets of the capitalist class and not into those of the workers. Far from
achieving the object intended, the working-class parties
at times tended to identify their interests with those of
the colonial peoples and the imperialist powers found
themselves engaged upon a conflict on two fronts, at
home with their own workers and abroad against the
growing forces of colonial liberation.

The postwar period inaugurated a very different colonial policy. A deliberate attempt was made to
divert colonial earnings from the wealthy class and use
them instead generally to finance the "Welfare State."
As will be seen from the examples given later, this was
the method consciously adopted even by those working-
class leaders who had before the war regarded the
colonial peoples as their natural allies against their capitalist enemies at home.[52]

Nkrumah's observation, from 1965, is extremely resonant
for critics of the Canadian pension system. The reduced
feasibility of business-as-usual required a pivot from the
structure described by Walter Rodney—colonial wealth
actively industrializing the imperial core—to a structure in

which the spoils of plunder were more equally distributed *within* the core. The building of welfare states founded on colonial theft entrenched intra-working-class stratification on a global scale.

The colonial relationship underpinning Global North welfare systems described by Nkrumah was obscured by degrees of separation—a corporation from the metropole extracted wealth in the colony and brought it back to the metropole; the state taxed that wealth and redistributed it to the working classes in the form of a welfare state. Analysts like Nkrumah had to parse out the relationship between imperialism in the periphery and welfare in the core. The neoliberal welfare state rooted in finance, however, has cut out the middleman altogether. Pension funds themselves own the corporations that take money from the Global South and put it towards welfare in the Global North, no taxation required! The welfare system *itself* is the vehicle of wealth extraction. Indeed, Kevin Skerrett's suggestion that Canadian pension funds are "masters of the neoliberal universe" could just as easily be recast as "masters of the neocolonial universe."

The irony of this is striking considering that infrastructure nationalism was a hallmark of Canadian politics throughout the twentieth century, such that even conservative politicians were waxing poetic on the floor of the House of Commons about the horrors of American capital. In one particular flashpoint debate, for instance, old-school Tory John Diefenbaker ripped the governing Liberals to pieces over their allowance of US ownership of a pipeline through Western Canada. Later, he would suggest that Canada was not truly an independent country if Americans owned all its critical infrastructure and resources.[53]

Canadian trade unions and leftists adamantly believed, through the 1960s and 1970s, that foreign ownership of

infrastructure made Canada functionally a colony of the
United States. The authors of the "Waffle Manifesto,"
activists and organizers on the left flank of the NDP, foregrounded these affirmations as a crucial part of their case
for a socialist Canada. Labour nationalism hit its fever
pitch as factory closures threatened Canada's industrial
core in the 1970s and 1980s. Prominent left economists
explicitly wedded programs for a socialist Canada to
claims that infrastructure nationalization would produce
an independent Canada.[54] Canadian trade unions strategically instrumentalized economic nationalism towards the
ends of guaranteeing public investment and subsidies for
factories threatened with closure.[55]

The pension funds ended up playing a role in this
nationalist moment. But whereas Canada used to be under-
stood as a victim of the global commodification of infrastructure, it now is unambiguously—through its pension
funds—one of the world's chief commodifiers. The historic
claim that Canada was a resource colony of the United
States always existed uncomfortably with the country's
position in the imperial core and its own ongoing colonialism of Indigenous Peoples, but by the 2000s it fully ceased
to be tenable.

Siphoning wealth from the Global South, it bears
emphasizing here, is the Canadian economy's entire modus
operandi. Considerable attention has been dedicated in
recent years to the role that Canadian corporations and
the Toronto Stock Exchange play in the global mining
economy. Sixty percent of mining companies are based
out of Toronto and have been responsible for violence and
exploitation worldwide, touching almost every corner of
the colonial world.[56] Whereas the wealth extracted through
mining winds up predominantly concentrated in the hands
of the few, the wealth extracted by pension funds ends up

more widely distributed. But it nevertheless produces class stratifications, widening the gulf between Canadian workers and their counterparts across the Global South.

Deborah Cowen refers to Bay Street, downtown Toronto's financial core, as representing the "finance-extractive-infrastructure nexus."[57] Banks, law firms, and traders come together to manage the enormous amounts of wealth extracted through Canadian imperialism. The big pension funds are right in the middle of it. Even as many of the infrastructures they finance are not extractive in the literal sense—they are not pulling resources out of the ground—they are still one of the mechanisms through which the money of the colonized ends up in the pockets of the colonizer.

THE LIMITS OF "SOCIAL INVESTMENT"

Climate catastrophe has made the composition of pension fund portfolios an imminent and urgent political issue. The energy networks described earlier are generally carbon intensive—oil pipelines, natural gas terminals, coal plants—and produce a pretty direct link between Ontario's retirement savings and the destruction of the planet. Efforts to decarbonize pension fund portfolios, unfortunately, have heretofore been Janus-faced. The corollary of the—positive, I should emphasize—push for public pension divestment from the fossil fuel economy has been a frequently uncritical celebration of any and all green investments.

In Canada, the main advocacy group for pension decarbonization has been a group called Shift: Action for Pension Wealth and Planet Health. Shift's primary aim has been to mobilize pension fund members to push their funds to divest from fossil fuels. As can perhaps be ascertained from the "Pension Wealth" component of the organization's name, the focus is on finding a common ground between profitable investment and eco-friendly strategies. The result, unfortunately, has largely been to celebrate a deepening of private ownership of critical utilities. The announcement of the Ontario Infrastructure Bank in November 2023, for instance, drew conditional applause from Shift, who wrote:

> There were few details about the OIB in today's fall economic statement, but this is a smart idea that incentivizes pension funds to invest in domestic infrastructure projects that can directly benefit their members. We'll be watching closely to ensure that the OIB invests in projects that reduce emissions and build a zero-carbon economy, particularly renewable energy, electricity transmission, energy efficiency and conservation, public transit and other climate solutions.[58]

The OMERS-OTPP-owned private energy utility Puget Sound Energy, similarly, was given acclaim by Shift for plans to build a wind farm in Montana on the basis that decarbonization is a profitable endeavour.[59] Shift's commentary on the 2023 mid-year results of OMERS, OTPP, the Caisse, and the CPP—in which they emphasized how investments in privatized renewable infrastructure had pushed fund growth—made their organizational book statement very explicit: "Investing in climate solutions is good for the planet and for our pensions."[60] There is money to be made in the green transition.

In simple terms, the dire and urgent need for green investment has turned some pension fund activists into inadvertent cheerleaders for privatization. The singular lens of the climate crisis puts blinders on to the wider social reverberations of infrastructure investments, while the dual framing of "pension wealth and planet health" reaffirms the base principles of the pension system as is. The effort to find a synthesis between pension fund rate of return and planetary survival means that for-profit utilities, as long as they are carbon neutral, win endorsements.

Unfortunately, this also takes on neocolonial dimensions. Given that many Global North countries have robust public power systems with enough political cachet to protect them from imminent privatization, many of the green investments celebrated by that segment of the pension advocate world are actually endeavours to ensure that the power grids of the decarbonized world are owned by private investors instead of by the state. Look no further than the OTPP's investments in Indian renewables discussed above—there are major growth opportunities in countries like India where, as Bardhan highlights, the entire renewable sector is already in private hands.[61] Investments in India have been specifically celebrated by Shift.[62]

The opportunities for lucrative investment in green infrastructure—of which there are many, especially given the shot in the arm "Bidenomics" has given the renewable industry in the United States—have pension funds drooling with anticipation of being at the forefront of a new carbon-neutral world. They want to get in on the ground floor of an infrastructure buildout that will give them monopoly rights over the next era of energy production. And so, with each passing year, the green portfolios of the pension funds get bigger, filled with infrastructure projects that should be built by the state.

This is not to say that every aspect of pension engagement in climate politics is a total lost cause. Nothing of the sort. Starving the fossil fuel economy of capital from institutional investors is a good thing. But we cannot prevent a mass-extinction event through a mass-privatization event. Even Shift's condemnation of OMERS and Thames

Water—which did explicitly highlight the tensions between the interests of a Kitchener municipal employee and a London resident—eventually fell back on the investment risk of nationalization, the suggestion that "bad practices" jeopardize reliable returns.[63] Privatized carbon-neutral utilities—the "perfect green investment"—are not the path forward in the climate crisis.

Nevertheless, there is a growing commitment from Canada's major pension funds to a better climate politics, and that definitely represents a positive. Since the early 2020s, OMERS and OTPP have been issuing bonds specifically for green investments, and the trendline has been pointing towards reduced pension support for the fossil fuel economy. Quebec's Caisse, meanwhile, has already begun actively divesting, having announced its shedding of new pipeline investments in late 2021.[64]

The push for Canada's pension funds to divest from the fossil fuel economy has long-standing antecedents in labour's approach to pension reform and the postindustrial era. Recall the Ontario Commission on Pension Investment contemplating South Africa when considering trusteeship models! Peter Drucker's provocative declaration of the era of "pension fund socialism" sparked energetic responses from labour economists looking for pathways to political change at a nadir in the power of organized labour. Jeremy Rifkin and Randy Barber's *The North Will Rise Again*, written in 1978 (and mentioned in chapter 1), saw pension funds as labour's response to deindustrialization *and* its best route to a socialist future. Based on a read of nationalization projects underway in West Germany and the United Kingdom and communist entry into government in France and Italy, Rifkin and Barber thought that the socialist future in the United States—though presumptuously proclaimed by

Drucker—could genuinely be imminent and that pension funds could be the agents of change.

Rifkin and Barber wrote on pension funds at a moment in which deindustrialization was ripping the US Midwest to pieces, shredding the labour movement (in their phrasing) more effectively than Pinkertons ever could. Their take was that trade unionists had become too comfy in boardrooms, and that a labour movement led by those leaders could never grapple with the runaway shop. Their conclusion was that the union-controlled pension funds could be wielded, in partnership with Democrat state governments, towards a re-industrialization strategy focused on community cooperatives and public enterprises.[65] To them, Drucker's proclamation of pension fund socialism had not been wrong—it had just been premature.

Within fifteen years of its release, Rifkin and Barber's vision of the "pension path to socialism" had been tempered by cold antilabour reality, and its optimism looks genuinely tragic. Work from Canadian pension activists, which developed heavily in the early 1990s, reveals a political moment—post-Reagan, post-Mulroney, and post-fall-of-the-Berlin-Wall—in which to speak optimistically of socialism was simply impossible. The main Canadian exponent of pension fund activism, economist Jack Quarter, instead grounded his work firmly in the old economic nationalist tradition discussed above. For Quarter, pension funds resulted in unions "crossing the line" and "blurring the division" between labour and capital, a new arrangement that the labour movement had to adapt to. His take was primarily that the goal of newly marketized funds such as OMERS and OTPP should be to "keep jobs in Canada" and fill vacuums left by capital flight.[66] The prevailing vision of class harmony was put very explicitly in the book's closing pages, where he wrote that "although this changed relationship to capital represents a departure from tradition, it is occurring without any ideological fervour and largely without any blueprint for social transformation."[67]

Pension fund activism, by the turn of the millennium, was top of mind for the highest echelons of both the Canadian and US labour movements. The American Federation of Labor and Congress of Industrial Organizations (AFL-CIO) sought to centralize labour's pension strategy and found a happy collaborator in its member union the United Steelworkers—together they set up the Heartland Labor Capital Network in 1995 to develop a long-term investment strategy for their pension funds. One outcome of this was a collection of essays articulating labour's vision of pension power in the twenty-first century. *Working Capital: The Power of Labor's Pensions* functions as a pure-form articulation of labour's approach to the pension question, a total distillation of how pensions came to be thought of as the "silver bullet" for a weakened labour movement. One line on the very first page speaks multitudes: the aim of pension fund activism should be to "advance the interests of all stakeholders in the economy in equal measure."[68] This notion of "what's good for capital can be good for labour" pervades a book in which job creation is viewed as the upper limit of pension activism.

Indeed, to read through forty years of pension investment literature is to watch organized labour's power—and the wider cachet of left-wing politics—diminish before your eyes. Rifkin and Barber's unambiguous optimism about the potential role of pension funds in a transformation of North American political economy was dashed upon the rocks of Reaganite reality, giving way to increasingly dreary dreams of labour shouting loud at shareholder meetings.

One text in this genre, *The Rise of the Working Class*

Shareholder, uses the biblical passage of David and Goliath as its epigraph, arguing that shareholder activism could be the stone in David's sling. Alas, its defeatist analysis presented pension politics as, in its best form, a handful of pebbles. Through coordinating shareholder votes (a process called proxy voting)—a form of "boardroom democracy," as it were—pension funds have been able to exercise some amount of influence on the internal operations of major corporations. The context is important—the 2018 book came out following the Supreme Court's decision in *Janus*, which made right-to-work national and made organized labour start planning its own funeral, something the author, David Webber, explicitly highlights—but the outlook is nevertheless bleak and sad. Using proxy voting to, say, reduce CEO salaries is valiant, but it is not transformative and sure does not defeat the Goliath of financial capitalism.

For decades, labour has been actively building social investment strategies to try to build a tool in their toolkit. Although "ESG" (a corporate-world shorthand for "Environmental, Social, Governance" considerations in investment choices) has become a more recent bugbear for the US right—a way for them to claim that even the most ardent capitalist secretly dreams of a Bolshevik Wall Street—it has been around for decades as a crucial articulation of labour's powerlessness. There exists an enormous network of union pension advocacy groups, from the aforementioned Shift and Heartland Labor to SHARE (a British Columbia–based group that focuses on coordinating shareholder leverage strategies) and the Committee on Workers' Capital (an initiative of the International Trade Union Confederation), which has built up since the 1980s—all committed, to varying degrees of radicalism, to a vision of "responsible" pension fund investment.

The reactionary right's war on ESG investment has put left critics of the pension system on the defensive. Fear of "woke capital" has driven right-wing politicians absolutely bananas and animated a legislative onslaught on the ability of public sector pensions to utilize ESG criteria when making investment decisions.[69] Partially in response to this, the US Democratic Party has firmly hitched its wagon to social investment. While the Democrats in the 1980s were unwilling to commit hard on a Rifkin-Barber vision of pension socialism, they are now fully invested in protecting public sector pensions' right to consider social criteria in their investment strategies.

Critics of pension fund capitalism, however, should resist the urge to be pigeon-holed into defending ESG criteria. There is no space for transformation within the financial system, and efforts to soften the edges function little more than to alleviate political pressure on that system. They are an effort to massage the contradictions of labour's imbrication in a political economy that requires them to root for the stock market to do well while also seeking to minimize harm.

A 2005 American Enterprise Institute-sponsored pamphlet, *Pension Fund Politics: The Dangers of Socially Responsible Investing*, argued that "fiduciary responsibility" and social investment—which they label "ideological vanity"—are contradictory.[70] Though their conclusion is to reify the former and chuck the latter aside, they—accidentally—correctly identify the heart of the issue. In a capitalist political economy, rate of return and social health are directly juxtaposed: there is no harmony between the profit motive and a good society.

This tension, unfortunately, has made much of the Canadian labour movement's approach to pension fund politics at best contradictory and at worst incoherent. A recognition of the plain reality that Canadians struggling to retire need good pensions means that unions (naturally and reasonably!) hope for maximal returns from the pension funds their members are part of, but, at the same time, a desire to stay true to labour movement values and maintain a key role in the current social movement climate results in them also condemning the roots of those maximal returns.

For the Canadian Auto Workers (now Unifor), the position was consistently to reaffirm that their sole responsibility for pensions was the value of the benefit they had bargained for. For them, "crossing the line" (to return to Jack Quarter's phrasing) was unconscionable. Such an approach—rooted, it must be said, in a very firm analysis of the respective roles of labour and capital—veers into the territory of "see no evil, hear no evil." Regardless of whether labour *wants to be* involved in the wider social question of the pension industry, they are—by virtue of a system they helped to create—wrapped up in it. You cannot be neutral on a moving train, especially when you are actively filling the engine with coal.

Even a union such as CUPE, for whom pension justice has been a political priority, falls into this trap. In spring 2021, the union published a deep dive into OMERS, lambasting the fund for a decade of investment returns that trailed the other big Canadian funds.[71] Their frustration is borne out of a concern that the fund's investment performance might result in benefit cuts or contribution increases. However, they also consistently and vocally criticize the fund when its portfolio has particularly socially corrosive characteristics that warrant additional attention.

Their obligations to their members push them to demand a higher rate of return from OMERS, while their aspirations towards social movement unionism lead them to an ardent (and earnest) critique of OMERS's portfolio.

But a higher rate of return for OMERS means that the screw is turned tighter on its investments—it means corners are cut by Thames Water, it means more of Ontario's health system ends up in private hands. In a perverse (and perhaps glib) way, society is likely better off when OMERS does poorly.

The Canadian pension system is predicated on a Faustian bargain that the potentially negative aspects of the investment portfolio are justified by the comfortable retirement afforded to workers who have earned it. With OMERS, the question is, are they even fulfilling the Faustian bargain? For other labour advocates within the pension system, the question has been, can we have the current system *without* the Faustian bargain? Can we have our retirements well-funded in the way they currently are *and* not have to worry about the negative impacts?

The answer is no! A financialized, socially neutral pension cannot exist. The prevailing vision of social investment essentially functions as the labour corollary to notions of "corporate social responsibility," which provide ideological cover to capitalism. The focus on using pension funds as a mechanism to preserve "accountability" in corporations and reward those that exhibit "good behaviour" shows a lack of interest in shifting the relationship between workers and employers. Instead, a vision of a socially harmonious capitalism—in which pension funds invest in firms that hire union and draw up master lists of "good companies"—carries through these proposals in the hopes that the rough edges of capitalist political economy can perhaps be sanded down. The mantra of job creation, without focus on the relationship between those jobs, the workers who fill them, and the bosses who direct them, results in a labour sign-off on a capitalist growth politics rather than a challenge to it. In the context of the climate crisis, this has been further coated over with the language of sustainability, with pension fund investments in green infrastructure celebrated rather than looked upon as a deepening of privatization. "Sustainable" investments have extended the logic of "the good capitalist" to climate catastrophe.

Ultimately, then, the strategy at play through social investment strategies—"woke capital" or otherwise—is essentially an endeavour to reconstruct the postwar labour compromise. For decades, labour and capital were able to have some harmony based on a system that promoted mutual growth. The dramatic shift in the balance of class forces since the 1970s unsettled that harmony, and approaches that hope to reproduce a system where capitalist economic growth is also good for workers cannot reproduce it.

And so, the notion of "shareholder activism" perhaps needs to be sidelined. So long as workers depend on the financial system for their retirements, there is no pathway for labour to wash its hands of that fact. The circle cannot be squared.

CONCLUSION

Seemingly disparate geographies are linked and bound to one another through the common tie of Canadian pension capital. The Ontario Municipal Employees Retirement System and the Ontario Teachers' Pension Plan take Ontario municipal labour global by tying workers' retirements to neocolonial enclosure of natural resources, utilities, and land. A Toronto bus driver's position in the global hierarchy of labour is reinforced and reproduced by the tolls taken from Indians commuting to work, Brazilians accessing clean drinking water, and Chileans keeping the lights on. Global rentierism puts welfare funds front and centre in the upward distribution of wealth to the imperial core.

Tracing the financial bonds of pension investment shows that the "labour of racial capitalism's infrastructures," to borrow Deborah Cowen's phrase, is not solely that which builds the infrastructure itself.[72] It is also the labour in Canada that benefits from the enclosure of everyday life in the Global South. These workers are the beneficiaries of a financial system segmented by race and class on a global scale. For these reasons, it is crucial that Canadian pension fund activists look globally. When leftists in Canada protest—as they have in recent years—against right-wing politics in India, Brazil, and beyond, attention must be drawn to how their own retirements benefit from those governments' sinister privatization agendas. Welfare here means exploitation there.

The labour movement has been vocal in its opposition to Canadian pension investment in Brazil, but it has been unsuccessful in putting on the pressure required to genuinely move the dial. CPP Investments did not end up buying shares in Eletrobras, but that was owing to their own cheapness and not to any statements released by unions. Teachers have been silent on their pension fund's complicity in Modi's privatization agenda. We have yet to see a real, sustained push by Canadian trade unionists against the investments of their pension funds.

Indeed, labour's activism in the pension realm has unfortunately been limited to those tools described by Webber as labour's "last, best, weapon." Activist investment strategies have gained some currency in the labour movement, with minimal impacts. Hopefully, the powerful pushes by Palestinian activists for divestment from Israel and weapons manufacturing in 2024 show the labour movement what a financial strategy with teeth can look like.

No amount of "social investment" can unravel the core contradiction at play in the financialized, postindustrial pension system. It is not just that "there is no ethical consumption under capitalism"—that capitalism itself is innately exploitative. This is true, but more specificity is required here. It is that the structure of postindustrial political economy means that the profitable investment a pension fund requires to meet its obligations can only be found in the same commodities pensioners themselves need to survive. Deindustrialization has foreclosed upon productive investment; all that remains is rent to be extracted from the necessities of the everyday.

Social investment will always be woefully insufficient. However, the criticism of social investment strategies should not mean that we in the labour movement and on the left should simply throw up our hands and resign ourselves to the status quo, as was the position of the Ontario Teachers Federation during the 1980s pension reform and of the Canadian Auto Workers in the 1990s. It means that our minds must turn to the crafting of alternative ways of funding retirement—or, of reconceptualizing retirement itself.

Building a Just City, Building a Just Retirement

How is it that Ontario can have some of the world's largest pension funds and yet still be the site of a retirement crisis? It is, in a sense, a recasting of the same question people have been asking since the beginning of industrial capitalism: How can there be poverty in the face of plenty? Hundreds of billions of dollars are invested in capital markets to finance a comfortable retirement at the same time as retirees live in poverty and fear.

COVID exposed the underlying fragility of the social infrastructures of both retirement and housing. Contemporary long-term care (LTC) facilities have taken the county poorhouse of which the London schoolteacher in 1924 was so afraid and turned it into a profit machine. The pandemic tore through Ontario's nursing homes, killing almost four thousand people in genuinely grim circumstances. Profit imperatives had undercut pandemic preparation by slashing staffing and reducing access to protective equipment, putting seniors directly in harm's way. As the Ontario Long-Term Care COVID19 Commission put it, "This may be an excellent financial arrangement for the investors, but it is more difficult to understand why it is a suitable arrangement for resident care."[1] The old Poor Law model of siloing the disposable old has been harnessed and commodified.

Indeed, as Andre Picard outlined in his "post-pandemic" (a term I use with caution and hesitation) deep dive into the Canadian LTC system, eldercare has always been treated as an afterthought compared to the public Medicare system and thus has been left open for the private sector to feast upon.[2] The thousands of people who died in Ontario's LTC facilities in 2020–21 merely punctuated and rendered acute a chronic, latent crisis—ask any personal support worker or nurse and they will tell you that nursing homes were a volcano waiting to erupt.

In a perverse irony, pension funds have come under particular scrutiny for their ownership of privatized LTC chains. The Public Service Alliance of Canada (PSAC), which represents workers in the federal public service, has drawn attention to their pension fund's ownership of Revera, an LTC chain in which 266 residents died between March and September 2020.[3] The OTPP, meanwhile, owns Amica, a chain of luxury retirement homes with locations in Ontario, British Columbia, and Alberta.[4]

The LTC industry is a global industry. The January 2022 release of *Les Fossoyeurs* [*The Gravediggers*] drew international attention to CPP Investments' 15 percent stake in European LTC chain Orpea, a company with a record of elder abuse and financial misappropriation, drawing ire from both the French and Canadian trade union movements.[5] While they are meant to be supporting retirees, pension funds have been capitalizing off the exploitation of the elderly.

And the retirement crisis is far from limited to the tragedies of the LTC system. Despite Canadian pension funds having over $2 trillion, retirees and retirees-to-be do not feel financially secure whatsoever, with survey after survey repeating the same chorus of "I don't think I'll ever make it to retirement."

The Faustian bargain made by the Canadian labour movement rests on the notion that the social consequences of fund investments are justified by the retirement support a solid pension provides. But we are not even getting that support! Everything bad about a financialized pension system—the privatized infrastructure, the unaffordable housing, the LTC death traps—we have in spades, and yet still millions struggle to support themselves in retirement. The pension's role as a means to support the elderly has become absolutely secondary to its role as investment capital. More money in your grandparents' pockets equals less money to be put into capital markets.

Meanwhile, the summer of 2021 saw a flashpoint in Toronto's housing crisis. The eviction of a homeless encampment in the city's west end was resisted with vigour by both the dispossessed themselves and their allies in Toronto's social movements. This resistance was met with horrific and brutal violence from police—mass arrests, kettling, and pepper spray.[6] Police attacks on homeless encampments at Trinity Bellwoods and Lamport Stadium brought to a head a crisis that had been rendered acute by COVID-19. And those same cops who brutalized the homeless in Toronto are, through OMERS, co-owners of luxury properties just a few kilometres away. The ground troops of Toronto's housing crisis are also, through their pensions, among its beneficiaries. After a brief downward movement during the first part of COVID, Toronto's rental crisis has returned with a vengeance, with the homeless and precariously housed bearing the brunt of it.

In among the crises upon crises that have characterized the past few years of Canadian capitalism, pension funds have redoubled their commitment to real estate and infrastructure. A survey of pension fund managers in late 2022 found that 44 percent intend to increase asset allocations towards alternatives in the context of high inflation.[7] Real estate and infrastructure investments held asset portfolios afloat while stock market volatility was threatening to put a significant dent in fund balance sheets. Although the rise of work-from-home arrangements have made major impacts on the commercial real estate market (negatively impacting many major pension portfolios), there is little expectation of a serious reversal of the pro-alternative trends in the pension investment sector.

The crisis of everyday life, for both the elderly and the wider working class, is driven in part by the pension fund contradiction. Pensions have to be predatory because a steady rate of return is integral to the financing of retirement for beneficiaries. However, those predations end up undermining retirement security for the greater public, producing a cycle in which pension funds necessitate their own existence by helping to make retirement itself expensive.

Urban social movements have pitched class struggle in the age of neoliberal urbanism against the commodification of the necessities of life, fighting capital on the terrain of social reproduction. Following in the tradition of Henri Lefebvre, critical geographers have, since the 1970s, written extensively on the "right to the city" as the ultimate aim of social movements seeking transformation of everyday life in urban space.[8] Struggles against welfare reform and gentrification have energized urban class politics through the linkage of anticapitalist politics to a vision of new forms of urban life.[9]

In Chile, birthplace of neoliberal pension reform, resistance to the mandatory and private state pension scheme has been front and centre in a radical feminist movement that has driven the country's politics to the left. Protesters in the streets of Santiago demanded reforms to the pension system that had left them, their parents, and their grand-parents destitute in old age. Even in *Bloomberg,* commentators highlighted the private pension system as emblematic of the failures of neoliberalism in Chile. The individualized retirement accounts championed by Pinochet and taken as a model by right-wing advocates worldwide—the disciples of *Averting the Old Age Crisis*—were put forward in summer 2022 as "neoliberalism's badge of shame."[10] France, meanwhile, hit a level of near-revolutionary fervour not seen in quite some time in response to 2023 efforts by Emmanuel Macron to raise the retirement age.

The politics of "the right to the city," in which capital's conquest of the urban landscape is actively contested, has an important role for municipal labour unions. Struggles for social reproduction in urban space by necessity bring the labour forces engaged in those sectors into their political formations, given that attacks on welfare double as attacks on public sector labour. Teachers' struggles across North America point towards the incredible possibilities of a radical municipal labour politics, with unions such as the Chicago Teachers Union and the United Teachers of Los Angeles enmeshing themselves heavily in the politics of their respective cities.

Indeed, Ontario's social movements are already engaged in this sort of organizing work, and further labour involvement should be encouraged. The Ontario Coalition Against Poverty and Justice for Workers, the successor to the successful Fight for $15 and Fairness, actively wed a right-to-the-city politics with a very explicit class consciousness and labourism. Tenant strikes across Toronto in 2023—most notably that of the York-South Weston Tenant Union—have built up power in the city's precariously housed. But, despite Ontario having a serious union presence in its municipal welfare state, labour involvement in these formations has heretofore been fairly limited.

In 2022, Ontario's labour movement showed levels of energy that it has not since the days of Mike Harris. Doug Ford's heavy-handed usage of the Notwithstanding Clause in Bill 28 to attempt to impose a contract upon low-paid maintenance and support staff in the province's school system catalyzed a generational response. Days of illegal strike action and the credible threat of a cross-union general strike—not just from public sector unions but penetrating the private sector as well—caused a panicked retreat by the premier and his lackeys.

For those invested in a strong labour movement capable of moving the political dial in Ontario, the events of November 2022 represented a huge glimmer of hope. Faced with a pile of garbage from an incumbent majority government, the labour movement chose not to pin their hopes on protracted court cases but instead moved swiftly to get the Bill knocked aside through an illegal strike.

Though it is worth analyzing whether more could have been achieved in that moment of labour militancy, the more important question is whether or not that momentum will be maintained going forward. Ontario's labour movement has been showing new signs of life outside of that one flashpoint. Generationally high inflation has provided an opportunity for Canadian unions to push back against the longer term issues of wage erosion, increasing cost-of-living, and antiworker public policy.

Major strikes across sectors in 2023 have shown that the energy of fall 2022 was perhaps not an aberration within a broadly docile Ontario labour relations environment. Wage increases are at levels unseen since the financial crisis. The 110,000 federal government workers represented by PSAC went on strike for twelve days in May 2023 and came away with both decent wage increases and lump sum payments. Signifying raised expectations, workers at Metro grocery stores in Toronto rejected a settlement their union had negotiated and struck for weeks before reaching a deal that gave them rate raises in the amount of multiple dollars. Unifor bargained with the auto sector simultaneously with their US counterparts and walked away with a deal that front-loaded a 10 percent raise. Further underscoring heightened expectations is the fact that the deal only barely ratified.

The scale of this energy should not be overstated—it bears noting that the two biggest teachers unions, the Ontario Secondary School Teachers Federation and the Elementary Teachers Federation of Ontario, voluntarily agreed to forgo strike action in favour of contract arbitration—but Ontario's unions have vibrance. So far, that vibrance has been largely shaped by economic circumstances. The priority of combatting wage erosion has, understandably, made the immediate question of "how can I afford to eat" the primary focus of labour action. Can that energy expand into a wider critique of the social system, one that links the issues of an individual collective agreement negotiation to those faced by all workers? People are angry, and the labour movement needs to harness that anger and do politics with it.

Activism surrounding pension issues has, as yet, not been a significant part of this energy, although it has come up in other bursts—PSAC and Ontario tenant activists explicitly targeting PSP Investments for nursing home profiteering and foul eviction practices show that pensions are on the radar. But a fulsome analysis linking the pension funds to the web of antilabour politics in the province has yet to be strongly foregrounded in Ontario's nascent labour resurgence.

The right to a decent retirement has been won through struggle and needs to be actively defended from those who would see it destroyed. Just because there was little appetite to dismantle OMERS and OTPP in the 1980s does not mean that politicians and commentators are not licking their lips at the prospect of turning Ontario's huge retirement systems into DC funds. The recent overtures from federal Liberals and provincial Tories towards the big funds definitely show that political consensus on pensions is broadly similar now to what it was then—capitalism is better off with massive coordinated investment pools rather than with individual retirement accounts, even if the latter reduces state obligations—but also highlight a desire to commit even more to pension fund capitalism. Alberta's present efforts to leave the Canada Pension Plan further point towards political conflict over retirement savings and investment strategies.

When public sector pension fund portfolios are socially catastrophic, it gives ammunition to advocates on the hard right who would love nothing more than a full Chile-style dismantling of the pension system. The value of a public sector pension is a classic talking-point for anti-union politicians who rail against "greedy" teachers, and that pension being used for socially corrosive ends further feeds the (obviously incorrect) notion that public sector workers get "cushy" jobs at the expense of everyone else. Bill Tufts and Lee Fairbanks's 2011 book *Pension Ponzi*, glowingly boosted by the Canadian Federation of Independent Business, is the perfect example of a right-wing screed that uses the real problems of pension investment to justify an aggressive anti-union politics. The book's backcover blurb, punctuated by the heading "how much is your neighbour's retirement going to cost you?," gloriously epitomizes the usage of pensions as a wedge issue:

The 20% of Canadians belonging to public sector unions managed to negotiate bulletproof job security, salaries that far outstrip anything comparable in the private sector, and incredibly generous pensions . . . and the 80% of taxpayers who don't belong to a public sector union—most of whom have no true pension at all—get the privilege of paying for it all . . .

Some call it pension envy, some call it pension apartheid. We call it a Pension Ponzi plan, an unsustainable funnelling of money from one group of Canadians to another. Canadians are being bilked out of their hard-earned money and cheated of secure retirements in order to gold-plate the pensions of those who have engineered the system in their favour.[11]

Protecting the DB pension from those who would like to see it destroyed depends upon fighting to fix the DB pension. The problem with the pension system, as I hope I have made clear through this book, is not the public sector unions who are ensnared within it. The problem with the pension system is the privatization of social welfare.

And so, fixing the pension system requires a move from the labour movement against that process of privatization. CUPE's battle with OMERS, unfortunately, has not been fully interwoven with a wider class politics. But the political vision that Ontario's labour movement—and the Ontario School Board Council of Unions in particular—brought to the battle against the Notwithstanding Clause can now hopefully be extended to a wider vision of a just society in which the reproductive needs of workers are placed front and centre. Ontario's healthcare crisis—which I am certain will get worse between the time I finish this draft and the time someone reads it—reveals more clearly than anything the scale of the relation between the rights of public sector workers and the health of their communities.

It is in this way, unfortunately, that the fight against Bill 28 and the Notwithstanding Clause reveals the strategic error made by the labour movement in their approach to the Ford government's public sector wage suppression, Bill 124. By focusing their fighting energy on a protracted court battle—a tactic that does not necessitate organizing but simply lives or dies on the strengths and weaknesses of legal teams—Ontario's unions missed a massive opportunity for a reckoning with the antisocial right wing in the province and beyond. A street fight over Bill 124 would have afforded the labour movement an opportunity to make clear how the fortunes of public sector workers are the same as those of the wider community around them.

Although the fight of the Ontario education workers was the result of a year's worth of preparation by the union's rank-and-file, as wonderful journalism by Martin Lukacs and Emma Paling laid out, the struggle's escalation from a contract dispute to an existential fight for the survival of the labour movement came as a result of a trigger-happy politician overplaying his hand.[12] Had he used the conventional playbook of public sector labour relations—bargain in bad faith, force a strike, let it happen for a day or two, and then use back-to-work legislation—the result would not have been so epochal, the labour movement would not be so reinvigorated and reunited.

The lesson is that, when right-wing governments poke the bear, the bear has to respond. There will be more instances of class warfare that will provide opportunities to the labour movement to build popular support, *but* the labour movement must take those opportunities. The steady dismantling of Ontario's social safety net could be the crisis needed for public sector unions to come together with social movements and reassert the importance of urban social reproduction. It is through that struggle—for a decommodification of everyday life—that a revolution in the pension system can occur.

Municipal labour unions in the North American city have an integral role to play in linking workplace struggle to community struggle. At the same time, however, municipal labour unions are caught within a brutal contradiction. While seeking a transformative urban politics that imagines forms of social reproduction outside the market, they are also, through their pension funds, actively engaged in these same processes of commodification.

How do we get out of the mess that I have spent this entire book outlining? The easy answer is to suggest the expansion of the public pension system, the CPP, so as to reduce reliance on private pension coverage. This is, alas, unsatisfactory. Since the reforms of the 1990s, the CPP has been just as predatory as any private pension; expanding it would necessitate higher rates of exploitation to yield higher rates of return on investment, turning the screw tighter on those who are already negatively impacted by it. Indeed, the CPP's investment portfolio speaks for itself— privatized water in Latin America should not be the basis of a comfortable retirement in Canada.[13] As was the case for the Global North welfare systems of the twentieth century, neoliberal financialized welfare remains predicated upon imperial exploitation abroad. Security *here* needs exploitation *there,* a social relation obscured by those analyses of the pension system that focus on Canadian demographic trends.

Indeed, the global dimensions of this history are critical. Analysis of both real estate and infrastructure shows how, on a world scale, the welfare of Canadian workers hinges upon accumulation by dispossession in countries in the Global South. Rentier ownership of natural resources, land, and utilities in the postcolonial world provides the basis for a comfortable retirement for some workers in the metropole. No just retirement can have this as its underpinning.

But a radical pension politics must also recognize the validity of workers' concerns over the security of their pensions. Workers have struggled for decent pensions to guarantee their ability to retire, something all workers should be entitled to. Any political solution to the pension contradiction therefore requires more finesse than simply saying, "Burn the pension funds to the ground." We must disentangle pension funds from webs of extraction while simultaneously guaranteeing a safe and comfortable retirement to pensioners—no small task.

The root cause of the pension contradiction is the commodification of necessities. If we accept two premises—first, that the ultimate purpose of a pension fund is to enable the continuous reproduction of its beneficiaries upon retirement, and second, that the underlying goal of "the right to the city" is to transform urban life towards a universalized ability to reproduce oneself—then this tension can actually become a congruity. Ultimately, the underlying basis of the contradiction is shared between both the "pension fund revolution" and "the right to the city"—the commodification of social reproduction and the usage of welfare as a terrain of accumulation. Decommodified systems of reproduction would render pension funds ultimately unnecessary, as housing, medical care, or other requirements for retirees would not be tied to the market. Were the necessities of life—and therefore the necessities of retirement—detached from the market, the imperative of pension funds to achieve high returns, contingent upon wealth extraction, would be lessened. The tension could, in fact, dissolve.

The answer, then, is to fight for a politics in which those commodities that are necessary for retirement are untethered from the market, rendering a sizable pension unnecessary. If the reproductive needs of the elderly—healthcare, pharmaceuticals, food, and, indeed, *housing*—were taken care of through nonmarket social systems, workers could grow old without relying on a large pension—and, by extension, without relying on exploitative market investments to finance it. Workers in the public sector are crucial to this politics. The connections forged between workers and their communities enables the sorts of political formations that can compellingly push for an enhanced and expanded vision of the "public good," inclusive of the necessities of both retirement and wider social survival.

The history of the urban working class is filled with examples of radical unions taking on the decommodification of everyday life as a pivotal terrain of struggle. Only a few miles east of Hudson Yards, on the Lower East Side, the Amalgamated Dwellings stand as a monument to potential urban life outside of capitalism. One of multiple cooperative housing complexes built by the Amalgamated Clothing Workers of America in the 1920s, the houses were built not just to provide affordable housing in a neighbourhood that was internationally notorious for its poor conditions—they were also explicitly intended to be a physical demonstration of power. As Amalgamated President Sidney Hillman put it, they "demonstrated that there is enough power in the labour movement to abolish slums, to give labor housing that will make decent living possible. That . . . is an accomplished fact. It is not a theory."[14] Before the creation of welfare state structures in the 1930s and 1940s, labour unions forged institutions of social reproduction outside the parameters of the market, severing the bond between welfare and accumulation.

A key reason for the establishment of employer-based pension schemes in the first place was to kneecap the efforts on the part of community-oriented unions to forge alternative systems of social reproduction. But they are also a tool that can be turned back on capital and used to transform urban life altogether. The enormous sums of capital owned and controlled by public sector pension funds could, in tandem with their unions engaging in community class politics, be wielded to help produce systems of social reproduction outside the market. Investment in social housing, childcare, community health, and—critically—old-age care could make pension funds a critical tool in the production of an earnest "right to the city," an urban landscape liberated from the confines of commodification. The antidemocratic structure of pension funds makes this an immense undertaking, and control is far from a silver bullet. But democratic control combined with an *active politics of decommodification* could put a municipal labour movement and its retirement savings at the forefront of a transformative urban politics. They might be part of the engine of accumulation, but they also hold the power to destroy it.

What would it look like, say, if Oxford Properties and Cadillac Fairview transformed their real estate portfolios into rent-geared-to-income housing? If Canada Guaranty reoriented away from mortgage insurance and towards underwriting co-op development? Or if they simply attached conditions to their purchases of large volumes of government bonds! It would altogether transform the urban landscape in Canada and beyond. But only their beneficiaries—Ontario's municipal workers and teachers—have the power to force that to happen. Political organizing within Ontario's major public sector unions and its broader working-class movement can link pension politics into a wider vision of a just city, using worker ownership to build a utopian urban project. Pensions could strategically invest themselves into irrelevance, and we would all be the better for it. Labour can build good housing when they have the capital to do so.

The pension contradiction is one that cannot be ignored or sidestepped; rather, it must be obliterated. A world in which everyone can grow old in comfort relies on it.

NOTES

INTRODUCTION

1   Natalie Wong, "Hudson Yard's $25 Billion Project Caps Global Push for Oxford," *Bloomberg*, March 6, 2019.

2   All monetary values in this book are in CAD, unless indicated otherwise.

3   Samuel Stein, "Forget 'Machine for Living in'–Hudson Yards Is a Machine for Investing in," *The Guardian*, March 15, 2019.

4   Sharon Zukin, "The City as a Landscape of Power: London and New York as Global Financial Capitals," in *The Global Cities Reader*, ed. Neil Brenner and Roger Keil, The Routledge Urban Reader Series (New York: Routledge, 2006), 137–46.

5   Julian Brash, *Bloomberg's New York: Class and Governance in the Luxury City*, Geographies of Justice and Social Transformation 6 (Athens: University of Georgia Press, 2011).

6   Kim Moody, *From Welfare State to Real Estate: Regime Change in New York City, 1974 to the Present* (New York: New Press, 2007).

7   Oxford Properties Group, "Oxford at a Glance," 2020, oxfordproperties.com.

8   CDPQ, "Mayor, Local Elected Officials, and Tenant Leaders Announce 20 Year Agreement with Blackstone and Ivanhoe Cambridge to Protect Middle Class Housing at Stuyvesant Town and Peter Cooper Village," October 20, 2015, cdpq.com.

9   OTPP, *2010 Annual Report* (Toronto, 2010); OTPP, *2020 Annual Report* (Toronto, 2020).

10 Statistics Canada, Table 11-10-0084-01, "Trusteed Pension

Funds, Value of Assets by Sector, Quarterly (x 1,000,000),"
(Government of Canada), accessed July 14, 2024,
statcan.gc.ca.

11 Task Force on the Investment of Public Sector Pension Funds,
In Whose Interest? (Toronto, 1987), 129, 188; OTPP, 2023
Annual Report (Toronto, 2023); OMERS, 2023 *Annual
Report* (Toronto, 2023).

12 Statistics Canada, Table 11-10-0085-01, "Trusteed Pension
Funds. Value of Assets by Foreign and Domestic Holdings,
Quarterly (x 1,000,000)." (Government of Canada), accessed
July 14, 2024, statcan.gc.ca.

13 "Maple Revolutionaries," *The Economist*, March 3, 2012.

14 Alex Mazer, Jonathan Weisstub, and Mahmood Nanji,
"The Evolution of the Canadian Pension Model: Practical
Lessons for Building World-Class Pension Organizations"
(Washington, D.C.: World Bank, 2017), 4.

15 Statistics Canada, Table 11-10-0084-01, "Trusteed Pension
Funds, Value of Assets by Sector, Quarterly (x 1,000,000)."
(Government of Canada), accessed July 14, 2024,
statcan.gc.ca.

16 Brett Christophers, *Rentier Capitalism: Who Owns the
Economy, and Who Pays for It?* (New York: Verso, 2020).

17 David Harvey, *The Limits to Capital* (London:
Verso, 2018), 379.

18 Raquel Rolnik, *Urban Warfare: Housing under the Empire of
Finance*, trans. Felipe Hirschhorn (London: Verso, 2019), 5.

19 Harvey, *Limits to Capital*, 244, 379.

20 Harvey, *Limits to Capital*, 379.

21 Tom Slater, "The Eviction of Critical Perspectives from
Gentrification Research," *International Journal of Urban
and Regional Research* 30, no. 4 (December 2006): 737–57,
doi: 10.1111/j.1468-2427.2006.00689.x.

22 For typical texts of this literature, see Archon Fung, Tessa
Hebb, and Joel Rogers, eds., *Working Capital: The Power
of Labor's Pensions* (Ithaca, NY: ILR Press, 2001); Isla
Carmichael, *Pension Power: Unions, Pension Funds, and
Social Investment in Canada* (Toronto: University of Toronto
Press, 2005); and David Webber, *The Rise of the Working-
Class Shareholder: Labor's Last Best Weapon* (Cambridge,
MA: Harvard University Press, 2018).

23 Gordon L. Clark, *Pension Fund Capitalism* (Oxford, UK: Oxford University Press, 2000); Richard Lee Deaton, *The Political Economy of Pensions: Power, Politics, and Social Change in Canada, Britain, and the United States* (Vancouver: University of British Columbia Press, 1989). For analysis of infrastructure, see Kevin Skerrett, "Pension Funds, Privatization, and the Limits to 'Workers Capital,'" *Studies in Political Economy* 99, no. 1 (January 2, 2018): 20–41, doi: 10.1080/07078552.2018.1440986.

24 Statistics Canada, Table 11-10-076-01, "Trusteed Pension Funds, Value of Assets by Sector, Quarterly" (Government of Canada), accessed November 20, 2020, doi: 10.25318/1110007601-ENG; Statistics Canada, Table 11-10-084-01, "Trusteed Pension Funds, Value of Assets by Sector, Quarterly" (Government of Canada), accessed June 17, 2024, statcan.gc.ca.

25 Oxford Properties Group, "Oxford at a Glance," 2020, oxfordproperties.com; Cadillac Fairview, "Our Portfolio," 2020, cadillacfairview.com.

26 Meg Luxton, "Feminist Political Economy and Social Reproduction," in *Social Reproduction: Feminist Political Economy Challenges Neo-Liberalism*, eds. Meg Luxton and Kate Bezanson (Montreal: McGill-Queens University Press, 2006), 36.

27 Tithi Bhattacharya, "Mapping Social Reproduction Theory," in *Social Reproduction Theory: Remapping Class, Recentering Oppression*, ed. Tithi Bhattacharya (London: Pluto Press, 2017), 1–20.

28 Gabriel Winant, *The Next Shift: The Fall of Industry and the Rise of Health Care in Rust Belt America* (Cambridge, MA: Harvard University Press, 2021).

29 Jane McAlevey, *No Shortcuts: Organizing for Power in the New Gilded Age* (New York: Oxford University Press, 2018), 28.

30 Karl Marx, *Capital: A Critique of Political Economy*, trans. Ben Fowkes, (London: Penguin Books),"Part 8: Primitive Accumulation."

31 Alan Sears, *Retooling the Mind Factory: Education in a Lean State* (Aurora, ON: Garamond Press, 2003); Nancy Fraser, "Between Marketization and Social Protection," in *Fortunes*

of Feminism: From State-Managed Capitalism to Neoliberal Crisis (New York: Verso Books, 2020); Wendy Brown, "What Exactly Is Neoliberalism?," interview by Timothy Shenk, Dissent, April 2, 2015, dissentmagazine.org.

32 Leonard Marsh, *Report on Social Security for Canada*, Canada Commons, 1943, 140.

33 Serap Saritas Oran, "Pensions and Social Reproduction," in Bhattacharya, *Social Reproduction Theory*, 164.

34 Gøsta Esping-Andersen, *The Three Worlds of Welfare Capitalism* (Princeton, NJ: Princeton University Press, 1990).

35 John C. Bacher, *Keeping to the Marketplace: The Evolution of Canadian Housing Policy* (Montreal: McGill-Queens University Press, 1989).

36 Kenneth Bryden, *Old Age Pensions and Policy-Making in Canada*, Canadian Public Administration Series (Montreal: McGill-Queens University Press, 1974).

37 Melinda Cooper, *Family Values: Between Neoliberalism and the New Social Conservatism*, Near Futures (New York: Zone Books, 2017); Nancy Fraser, "Crisis of Care?," in Bhattacharya, *Social Reproduction Theory*.

38 Fraser, "Crisis of Care?," 35.

39 See, for example, Steven Tufts, "Community Unionism in Canada and Labor's (Re)Organization and Space," *Antipode* 30, no. 3 (1998): 227–50; Simon Black, *Social Reproduction and the City: Welfare Reform, Child Care, and Resistance in Neoliberal New York*, Geographies of Justice and Social Transformation, volume 49 (Athens: University of Georgia Press, 2020); Steven Tufts, "World Cities and Union Renewal," *Geography Compass* 1, no. 3 (May 2007): 673–94, doi: 10.1111/j.1749-8198.2007.00031.x. The writings of David Camfield are particularly useful here: David Camfield, "Sympathy for the Teacher: Labour Law and Transgressive Workers' Collective Action in British Columbia, 2005," *Capital and Class* 33, no. 3 (2009): 81–107; David Camfield, "Renewing the Study of Public Sector Unions in Canada," *Socialist Studies/Études Socialistes* 1, no. 2 (January 2, 2009), doi: 10.18740/S4D60N; David Camfield, "The 'Great Recession,' the Employers' Offensive, and Canadian Public Sector Unions."

40 McAlevey, *No Shortcuts,* 28.

41 David Harvey, *Social Justice and the City* (London: Edward Arnold, 1973), 137. Emphasis his. My many thanks to Jason Spicer for introducing me to this passage.

ONE: MAKING A PUBLIC-PRIVATE-PUBLIC WELFARE STATE

1   Jeanne L. Wellhauser, "Brief to the Task Force on the Investment of Public Sector Pension Funds," December 11, 1986, RG6-104, Box 315, File: Briefs, Provincial Archives of Ontario.

2   Ontario Expert Commission on Pensions, *A Fine Balance: Safe Pensions–Affordable Plans–Fair Rules* (Toronto: Government of Ontario, 2008), 10.

3   Jennifer Klein, *For All These Rights: Business, Labor, and the Shaping of America's Public-Private Welfare State* (Princeton, NJ: Princeton University Press, 2003).

4   Cited in James Struthers, *The Limits of Affluence: Welfare in Ontario, 1920-1970,* Ontario Historical Studies Series (Toronto: University of Toronto Press, 1994), 50.

5   Struthers, *Limits of Affluence,* 51.

6   Struthers, *Limits of Affluence,* chapter 2, 50–76.

7   Cited in Bryden, *Old Age Pensions,* 24, 78.

8   Klein, *For All These Rights,* 3.

9   Marsh, *Report on Social Security,* 251.

10 Neil Tudiver, "Forestalling the Welfare State: The Establishment of Programmes of Corporate Welfare," in *The "Benevolent" State: The Growth of Welfare in Canada,* eds. Allan Moscovitch and Jim Albert (Toronto: Garamond Press, 1987), 186–204.

11 Michael A. McCarthy, *Dismantling Solidarity: Capitalist Politics and American Pensions since the New Deal* (Ithaca, NY: ILR Press, 2017).

12 Esping-Andersen, *Three Worlds of Welfare Capitalism,* 43, 66.

13 H. M. Grant, "Solving the Labour Problem at Imperial Oil: Welfare Capitalism in the Canadian Petroleum Industry, 1919-29," *Labour / Le Travail,* no. 41 (Spring 1998): 69–95.

14 See Blackburn, *Banking on Death,* 79–80 for a succinct definition.

15 Bryden, *Old Age Pensions,* 165.

16 Bryden, *Old Age Pensions,* 188.

17 Nancy Fraser, "After the Family Wage: A Postindustrial Thought Experiment," in *Fortunes of Feminism*, 151–87.

18 Peter F. Drucker, *The Unseen Revolution: How Pension Fund Socialism Came to America*, 1st ed (New York: Harper & Row, 1976).

19 Drucker, *Unseen Revolution*.

20 Deaton, *Political Economy of Pensions*, 216.

21 Stephanie Ross and Larry Savage, eds., *Public Sector Unions in the Age of Austerity* (Halifax, NS: Fernwood Publishing, 2013), 11.

22 Stephanie Ross, "The Making of CUPE" (PhD diss., York University, 2005), 437.

23 See Blackburn, *Banking on Death*, 79–80.

24 Teresa Ghilarducci, *When I'm Sixty-Four: The Plot against Pensions and the Plan to Save Them* (Princeton, NJ: Princeton University Press, 2018), 90, 129.

25 Ontario Expert Commission on Pensions, *A Fine Balance*.

26 Steven C. High, *Industrial Sunset: The Making of North America's Rust Belt, 1969–1984* (Toronto: University of Toronto Press, 2003), 138.

27 High, *Industrial Sunset*, 183–5.

28 See Blackburn, *Banking on Death*, chapter 2.

29 Statistics Canada, "Registered Pension Plans (RPPs), Active Members and Market Value of Assets by Size of Plan Assets" (Government of Canada), accessed November 20, 2020, doi: 10.25318/1110012401-ENG.

30 Statistics Canada, "Registered Pension Plans."

31 Statistics Canada, "Registered Pension Plans."

32 Task Force on the Investment of Public Sector Pension Funds, *In Whose Interest*, 309, vii.

33 James R. Fisher, "Letter to Malcolm Rowan," June 23, 1987, RG6-104, Box 316, File: Niagara Seminar, Provincial Archives of Ontario. Emphasis his.

34 Task Force on the Investment of Public Sector Pension Funds, *In Whose Interest*, 129, 188.

35 Teachers Superannuation Commission, "Submission to the Task Force on the Investment of Public Sector Pension Funds," 1986, RG6-104, Box 313, File: Submissions, Provincial Archives of Ontario.

36 David Peterson, "Legislative Debates Quotes Re: Public

Sector Pensions and the CPP," n.d., RG6-104, Box 313, File: Statements, Ontario government, Provincial Archives of Ontario.

37 Task Force on the Investment of Public Sector Pension Funds, *In Whose Interest*, 1.

38 Task Force on the Investment of Public Sector Pension Funds, "Investment of Public Sector Pension Funds," July 10, 1987, RG6-104, Box 308, File: Briefings, Provincial Archives of Ontario.

39 Deaton, *Political Economy of Pensions*, 185.

40 Kim Phillips-Fein, *Fear City: New York's Fiscal Crisis and the Rise of Austerity Politics*, First Edition (New York: Metropolitan Books, Henry HOH and Company, 2017), 201, 153.

41 "A Summary of the Royal Commission on Status of Pensions in Ontario, 1981/82," January 29, 1987, RG6-104, Box 308, File: Briefings, Provincial Archives of Ontario.

42 Pension Investment Association of Canada, "Brief to the Task Force on the Investment of Public Sector Pension Funds," May 13, 1987, RG6-104, Box 315, File: Briefs, Provincial Archives of Ontario.

43 "Summary of the Royal Commission, 1981/82."

44 "Summary of the Royal Commission, 1981/82," emphasis mine.

45 "Summary of the Royal Commission, 1981/82."

46 Malcolm Rowan, "Memorandum to Dr Bryne Purchase, Assistant Deputy Minister & Chief Economist, Office of Economic Policy Re: Ontario's Public Sector Pension Funds," January 12, 1987, RG6-104, Box 313, File: Task Force Correspondence, Provincial Archives of Ontario. Emphasis mine.

47 Task Force on the Investment of Public Sector Pension Funds, *In Whose Interest?*, 14.

48 Blackburn, *Banking on Death*, 74.

49 World Bank, *Averting the Old Age Crisis*, 17.

50 Lucy Nicholson et al., "Letter to David Peterson Re: Public Sector Pensions Advisory Board, Task Force on the Investment of Public Sector Pension Funds," October 9, 1986, RG6-104, Box 313, File: Public Sector Pension Advisory Board, Provincial Archives of Ontario.

51 Task Force on the Investment of Public Sector Pension Funds, "Presentation to the Financial Community, List of Attendees," December 1, 1986, RG6-104, Box 313, File: Presentations, Provincial Archives of Ontario; Business Committee on Pension Policy, "Minutes of Meeting," February 25, 1987, RG6-104, Box 313, File: Presentations, Provincial Archives of Ontario; Task Force on the Investment of Public Sector Pension Funds, "Notes for a Presentation to Pension Investment Association of Canada," January 8, 1987, RG6-104, Box 313, File: Presentations, Provincial Archives of Ontario.

52 Nicholson et al., "Letter to David Peterson."

53 Doug McAndless, "Letter to David Peterson Re: Investment of Public Sector Pension Funds," September 30, 1986, RG6-104, Box 313, File: Task Force Correspondence, Provincial Archives of Ontario.

54 Drucker, *The Unseen Revolution*.

55 Sanford M. Jacoby, *Labor in the Age of Finance: Pensions, Politics, and Corporations from Deindustrialization to Dodd-Frank* (Princeton, NJ: Princeton University Press, 2021).

56 Jeremy Rifkin and Randy Barber, *The North Will Rise Again: Pensions, Politics and Power in the 1980s* (Boston: Beacon Press, 1978).

57 Jack Quarter, *Crossing the Line: Unionized Employee Ownership and Investment Funds* (Toronto, ON: James Lorimer, 1995).

58 Ian Thomas MacDonald and Mathieu Dupuis, "Managing Workers' Capital? Limits and Contradictions of Labour Investment Funds," *Economic and Industrial Democracy*, 42, no. 3 (September 2018): 4, doi: 10.1177/0143831X18793025.

59 Jacques Parizeau, "Letter to Malcolm Rowan," March 11, 1987, RG6-104, Box 316, File: Niagara Seminar, Provincial Archives of Ontario. Task Force on the Investment of Public Sector Pension Funds, "Notes for a Presentation to Pension Investment Association of Canada," January 8, 1987, RG6-104, Box 313, File: Presentations, Provincial Archives of Ontario.

60 Task Force on the Investment of Public Sector Pension Funds, *In Whose Interest?*, 201.

61 Toronto Society of Financial Analysts, "Brief to the Task

Force on the Investment of Public Sector Pension Funds," April 13, 1987, RG6-104, Box 315, File: Briefs, Provincial Archives of Ontario.

62 H. R. Akehurst, "Letter to the Malcolm Rowan Task Force on Investment of Public Sector Pensions," December 16, 1987, RG6-104, Box 308, File: Municipal letters re: OMERS, Provincial Archives of Ontario. This letter is merely the first in alphabetical order—it is one of dozens.

63 Task Force on the Investment of Public Sector Pension Funds, *In Whose Interest?*, 1.

64 James Campbell, "The NDP's Plan to Betray Pensioners," *Financial Times*, July 22, 1991, Fonds 1011: CUPE Local 79, Series 1844: Anne Dubas records, File 372: OMERS 1991-92, City of Toronto Archives.

65 CUPE Ontario, "Investment Policy for Public Sector Pension Funds," October 4, 1991, Fonds 1011: CUPE Local 79, Series 1844: Anne Dubas records, File 131: City pension negotiation, City of Toronto Archives.

66 Roy A. Schotland, "Presentation to Niagara Seminar," June 16, 1987, RG6-104, Box 316, File: Niagara Seminar, Provincial Archives of Ontario. Emphasis his.

67 Task Force on the Investment of Public Sector Pension Funds, *In Whose Interest?*, 2.

68 Task Force on the Investment of Public Sector Pension Funds, "Investment of Public Sector Pension Funds," July 10, 1987, RG6-104, Box 308, File: Briefings, Provincial Archives of Ontario.

69 Malcolm Rowan, "Notes on Social Investing," n.d., RG6-104, Box 313, File: Social Investing, Provincial Archives of Ontario.

70 Task Force on the Investment of Public Sector Pension Funds, "Public Sector Pension Reform: A Proposed Implementation Strategy," October 25, 1987, RG6-104, Box 308, File: Briefings, Provincial Archives of Ontario.

71 Don Ezra, "Notes on My Session at the Ontario Task Force Seminar (Niagara)," June 18, 1987, RG6-104, Box 316, File: Niagara Seminar, Provincial Archives of Ontario.

72 Malcolm Rowan, "Notes on Social Investing," n.d., RG6-104, Box 313, File: Social Investing, Provincial Archives of Ontario.

73 Malcolm Rowan, "Memorandum to Robert Carman, Secretary to the Cabinet, Re: Pension Fund Investment in South Africa," December 16, 1986, RG6-104, Box 313, File: Task Force Correspondence, Provincial Archives of Ontario.

74 Task Force on the Investment of Public Sector Pension Funds, "Investment of Public Sector Pension Funds."

75 Task Force on the Investment of Public Sector Pension Funds, *In Whose Interest?*, 7.

76 Quinn Slobodian, *Globalists: The End of Empire and the Birth of Neoliberalism* (Cambridge, MA: Harvard University Press, 2018).

77 Government of Ontario, "Bill 206: An Act to Revise the Ontario Municipal Employees Retirement System" (2006).

78 Blackburn, *Banking on Death*, 73, 227.

79 Mitchell A. Orenstein, *Privatizing Pensions: The Transnational Campaign for Social Security Reform* (Princeton, NJ: Princeton University Press, 2008), 27.

80 World Bank, ed., *Averting the Old Age Crisis: Policies to Protect the Old and Promote Growth* (New York, 1994). Blackburn, *Banking on Death*, discusses *Averting the Old Age Crisis* from 229–236.

81 Blackburn, *Banking on Death*, chapters 5 and 6, 279–413.

82 Bruce Little, *Fixing the Future: How Canada's Usually Fractious Governments Worked Together to Rescue the Canada Pension Plan* (Toronto: University of Toronto Press, 2008).

83 "Panel Discussion," *Benefits Canada*, March 2009.

84 "Crisis? What Crisis?," *Benefits Canada*, February 2010.

85 Government of Ontario, "Teachers' Pension Act," C92 § (1989).

86 Roy A. Schotland, "Letter to Malcolm Rowan," June 24, 1987, RG6-104, Box 316, File: Niagara Seminar, Provincial Archives of Ontario.

87 Keith Ambachtsheer, "The Ambachtsheer Letter," February 1988, RG6-104, Box 308, File: Correspondence re: task force, Provincial Archives of Ontario.

TWO: PENSIONS, PROPERTY, AND POVERTY

1   David Harvey, *Social Justice and the City* (London: Edward Arnold, 1973), 203.

2   Neil Smith, *The New Urban Frontier: Gentrification and the Revanchist City* (New York: Routledge, 1996).

3   Cited in Bryan D. Palmer and Gaétan Héroux, *Toronto's Poor: A Rebellious History* (Toronto, ON: Between the Lines, 2016), 297.

4   Brian O'Keefe, "Where Did the Rae Government Fail?," *News "n" Views: CUPE Local 79*, June 1994, Fonds 1011: CUPE Local 79, Series 1833, File 17, City of Toronto Archives.

5   Julie-Anne Boudreau, Roger Keil, and Douglas Young, *Changing Toronto: Governing Urban Neoliberalism* (Toronto: University of Toronto Press, 2009), 59; *Socialist Studies* 7, no. 1/2 (Spring/Fall 2011): 95–115; Greg Albo and Bryan M. Evans, *Divided Province Ontario Politics in the Age of Neoliberalism* (Montreal: McGill-Queens University Press, 2019), deslibris.ca; Bryan Mitchell Evans and Carlo Fanelli, eds., *The Public Sector in an Age of Austerity: Perspectives from Canada's Provinces and Territories* (Montreal: McGill-Queens University Press, 2018); Kendra Coulter, "Women, Poverty Policy, and the Production of Neoliberal Politics in Ontario, Canada," *Journal of Women, Politics & Policy* 30, no. 1 (January 2009): 23–45, doi: 10.1080/15544770802367788; and Kate Bezanson, "The Neo-Liberal State and Social Reproduction: Gender and Household Insecurity in the Late 1990s," in *Social Reproduction: Feminist Political Economy Challenges Neo-Liberalism*, ed. Kate Bezanson and Meg Luxton (Montreal: McGill-Queens University Press, 2006), 173–214; Carlo Fanelli, *Megacity Malaise: Neoliberalism, Public Services and Labour in Toronto* (Winnipeg, MB: Fernwood Publishing, 2016); Ian Thomas MacDonald, ed., *Unions and the City: Negotiating Urban Change* (Ithaca, NY: ILR Press, 2017); Roger Keil, "Third Way Urbanism: Opportunity or Dead End?," *Alternatives: Global, Local, Political* 25, no. 2 (April 2000): 247–67, doi: 10.1177/030437540002500204; Stefan Kipfer and Roger Keil, "Toronto Inc? Planning the Competitive City in the New Toronto," *Antipode* 34, no. 2 (March 2002): 227–64, doi: 10.1111/1467-8330.00237; and Julie-Anne Boudreau, Roger Keil, and Douglas Young, *Changing Toronto: Governing Urban Neoliberalism* (Toronto: University of Toronto Press, 2009).

6   Boudreau, Keil, and Young, *Changing Toronto,* 59.

7   Palmer and Heroux, *Toronto's Poor,* 352.

8   Palmer and Heroux, *Toronto's Poor,* 299.

9   Fanelli, *Megacity Malaise,* 24.

10 Fanelli, *Megacity Malaise,* 26.

11 Andy Hanson, "Not in Their Classrooms: Class Struggle and Union Strength in Ontario's Elementary Teachers' Unions, 1970–1998" (PhD diss., Trent University, 2013), 348.

12 Hanson, "Not in Their Classroom," 348.

13 Bezanson, "The Neo-Liberal State," 174.

14 Bezanson, "The Neo-Liberal State," 182.

15 Hanson, "Not in Their Classroom"; David Rapaport, *No Justice, No Peace: The 1996 OPSEU Strike against the Harris Government in Ontario* (Montreal: McGill-Queens University Press, 1999).

16 Hanson, "Not in Their Classroom"; Rapaport, *No Justice, No Peace*; Douglas Nesbitt, "Days of Action: Ontario's Extra-Parliamentary Opposition to the Common Sense Revolution, 1995–1998" (PhD diss., Queens University, 2018).

17 David Kidd, "Metro Days of Action," *News "n" Views: CUPE Local 79,* January 1997, Fonds 1011: CUPE Local 79, Series 1833, File 17, City of Toronto Archives.

18 Simon Black, *Social Reproduction and the City: Welfare Reform, Child Care, and Resistance in Neoliberal New York,* Geographies of Justice and Social Transformation, volume 49 (Athens: University of Georgia Press, 2020).

19 Rianne Mahon, "Rescaling Social Reproduction: Childcare in Toronto/Canada and Stockholm/Sweden," *International Journal of Urban and Regional Research* 29, no. 2 (June 2005): 341–57.

20 Gregory Suttor, *Still Renovating: A History of Canadian Social Housing Policy,* McGill-Queens Studies in Urban Governance 6 (Montreal: McGill-Queens University Press, 2016).

21 Alan Walks and Dylan Simone, "Neoliberalization through Housing Finance, the Displacement of Risk, and Canadian Housing Policy: Challenging Minsky's Financial Instability Hypothesis," *Research in Political Economy* 31 (2016): 65.

22 Jonathan Greene, "Urban Restructuring, Homelessness, and Collective Action in Toronto, 1980–2003," *Urban*

History Review 43, no. 1 (May 22, 2015): 21–37, doi: 10.7202/1030805ar.

23   Palmer and Heroux, *Toronto's Poor,* chapter 5, 291–428.

24   Kipfer and Keil, "Toronto Inc?"

25   David Harvey, "From Managerialism to Entrepreneurialism: The Transformation in Urban Governance in Late Capitalism," *Geografiska Annaler: Series B, Human Geography* 71, no. 1 (April 1989): 3–17, doi: 10.1080/04353684.1989.11879583.

26   Jamie Peck, "Austerity Urbanism: American Cities under Extreme Economy," *City* 16, no. 6 (December 2012): 630, doi: 10.1080/13604813.2012.734071.

27   David Camfield, "The 'Great Recession,' the Employers' Offensive, and Canadian Public Sector Unions," *Socialist Studies* 7, no. 1/2 (Spring/Fall 2011): 95–115.

28   Hanson, "Not in Their Classroom," 400.

29   Roger Keil, "'Common-Sense' Neoliberalism: Progressive Conservative Urbanism in Toronto, Canada," in *Spaces of Neoliberalism*, eds. Neil Brenner and Nik Theodore (Chichester, UK: John Wiley & Sons, Ltd, 2012), 230–53, doi: 10.1002/9781444397499.ch10.

30   Smith, *New Urban Frontier.*

31   John David Hulchanski, University of Toronto, and Cities Centre, *The Three Cities within Toronto: Income Polarization among Toronto's Neighbourhoods, 1970–2005* (Toronto, ON: Cities Centre, University of Toronto, 2011), deslibris.ca.

32   Alan Walks, "Homeownership, Asset-Based Welfare, and the Neighbourhood Segregation of Wealth," *Housing Studies* 31, no. 7 (2016): 755–84.

33   Canadian Mortgage and Housing Corporation, "Housing Market Outlook: Canadian Metropolitan Areas," Housing Market Information, April 2024, gc.ca.

34   Harvey, *Social Justice and the City,* 157–9. My thanks to Robert Lewis for introducing me to this.

35   "Bigger = Better," *Benefits Canada*, February 2010.

36   "Bigger = Better."

37   Walks and Simone, "Neoliberalization through Housing Finance, 58.

38   Alan Walks, "Bailing out the Wealthy: Responses to the Financial Crisis, Ponzi Neoliberalism, and the City,"

Human Geography 3, no. 3 (November 2010): 60, doi: 10.1177/194277861000300303.

39   Task Force on the Investment of Public Sector Pension Funds, "Public Sector Pension Reform: A Proposed Implementation Strategy," October 25, 1987, RG6-104, Box 308, File: Briefings, Provincial Archives of Ontario.

40   Task Force on the Investment of Public Sector Pension Funds, *In Whose Interest?*, 188.

41   Ontario Municipal Employees Retirement Board, "Submission to the Pension Commission of Ontario Respecting Policy Recommendations for the Regulation of Pension Fund Investments," August 27, 1986, RG6-104, Box 313, File: Responses to Policy Recommendations for Regulation of Pension Fund Investments, Provincial Archives of Ontario.

42   Keith Ambachtsheer, "Put 25% into Real Estate," *Benefits Canada*, June 1982.

43   World Bank, ed., *Housing: Enabling Markets to Work; with Technical Supplements*, Washington, D.C., 1993.

44   Rolnik, *Urban Warfare*, 20–1.

45   D. Rausa Maurice, "Basel I and the Law of Unintended Consequences," *Bank Accounting and Finance* 17, no. 3 (April 2004): 20–27.

46   Andrea Davis, "OMERS Increases Real Estate Exposure," *Benefits Canada*, November 1999.

47   Caroline Cakebread, "Re-Assessing Real Estate," *Benefits Canada*, November 2001.

48   Jeff Sanford, "Ontario Teachers' Buy Cadillac Fairview," *Benefits Canada*, January 2000.

49   "Ontario Teachers' Buy Cadillac Fairview."

50   OMERS, *2011 Annual Report* (Toronto, ON, 2011), 6. OTPP, *2008 Annual Report* (Toronto, ON, 2008), 1.

51   Caroline Helbrunner and Jessica Bullock, "Pensions at Risk," *Benefits Canada*, October 2009.

52   David Burke and Claude Leblanc, "Double Vision," *Benefits Canada*, February 2009.

53   David Harvey, *Rebel Cities: From the Right to the City to the Urban Revolution* (London: Verso, 2012), especially chapter 2.

54   "Alternative Reality," *Benefits Canada*, October 2010.

55 "The Road to Recovery," *Benefits Canada*, December 2009.

56 Doug Watt, "Why Are Real Assets So Popular?," *Benefits Canada*, March 20, 2015, benefitscanada.com.

57 Tom Lappelainen, "Report Card on Alternatives," *Benefits Canada*, Fall 2009.

58 Jerry Moskowitz, "Under Construction," *Benefits Canada*, Fall 2009.

59 Watt, "Why Are Real Assets So Popular?"

60 Scot Blythe, "Why Pension Plans Are Investing in Alternatives," *Benefits Canada*, December 19, 2011, benefitscanada.com.

61 Walks, "Bailing out the Wealthy," 68.

62 Alan Walks and Brian Clifford, "The Political Economy of Mortgage Securitization and the Neoliberalization of Housing Policy in Canada," *Environment and Planning* 47 (2015): 1628.

63 Canada Guaranty, "About Us," 2022, canadaguaranty.ca.

64 Walks and Clifford, "Political Economy of Mortgage Securitization," 1629.

65 OTPP, "Ontario Teachers Announces Agreement to Acquire HomeEquity Bank," September 22, 2021, otpp.com.

66 Keeanga-Yamahtta Taylor, *Race for Profit: How Banks and the Real Estate Industry Undermined Black Homeownership*, Justice, Power, and Politics (Chapel Hill: University of North Carolina Press, 2019).

67 Walks and Simone, "Neoliberalism through Housing Finance," 57.

68 Walks, "Homeownership," 755–6.

69 Cooper, *Family Values,* especially chapter 3 "The Return of Inherited Wealth," 119–66.

70 Oxford Properties, "Lease with Us," 2022, oxfordproperties.com.

71 Cadillac Fairview, "Our Portfolio," 2022, cadillacfairview.com.

72 Haseena Manek, "Invested in Crisis," *Briarpatch Magazine*, August 2020, briarpatchmagazine.com.

73 Richard Warnica, "Already Controversial for Its Ownership of Revera, One of Canada's Largest Pension Plans Has Just Announced a $700-Million Joint Venture with an Architect of 'the Big Short,'" *Toronto Star*, February 6, 2021.

74 "PSP Displaces Tenants," pspdisplacestenants.com.

75 Rowland Atkinson, *Alpha City: How the Super-Rich Captured London* (London: Verso, 2020).

76 "OMERS in Joint Venture with the Queen's Property Firm," *Benefits Canada*, May 28, 2013.

77 "Oxford Properties Buys Watermark Place," *Benefits Canada*, October 6, 2010.

78 Julian Brash, *Bloomberg's New York: Class and Governance in the Luxury City* (Athens: University of Georgia Press, 2011).

79 Brash, *Bloomberg's New York.*

80 Brash, *Bloomberg's New York.*

81 Oxford Properties Group, "Hudson Yards," 2022, oxfordproperties.com.

82 Neil Demause, "New School Study Uncovers Another $1 Billion in Hudson Yards Subsidies," *Gothamist*, November 5, 2018.

83 Kriston Capps, "The Hidden Horror of Hudson Yards Is How It Was Financed," *CityLab*, April 12, 2019.

84 "Caisse Reinvesting in Quebec Energy Company, CPPIB and Oxford Selling Toronto Landmark," *Benefits Canada*, January 18, 2022, benefitscanada.com.

THREE: LOCAL LABOUR, GLOABL INFRASTRUCTURE

1 "Strategy Master Class," *Benefits Canada*, August 2011.

2 OTPP, "Infrastructure and Natural Resources Portfolio," accessed November 15, 2021, otpp.com.

3 OMERS, "Private Investing Portfolio," accessed November 15, 2021, omers.com.

4 Brett Christophers, *Our Lives in Their Portfolios: Why Asset Managers Own the World* (London: Verso, 2023).

5 Heather Whiteside, "Advanced Perspectives on Financialised Urban Infrastructures," *Urban Studies* 56, no. 7 (May 2019): 1479, doi: 10.1177/0042098019826022.

6 OMERS, "OMERS Infrastructure Announces Sale of Hospital and Long-Term Care Facility Portfolio to Plenary Group," November 14, 2019, omersinfrastructure.com.

7 Tom Fraser, "Canadian Pension Funds Are Financing the Exploitation of the Elderly," *Jacobin*, March 20, 2022, jacobin.com.

8   Paul W. Bennett, "Reinventing the Building of Schools: The Real Legacy of Public-Private-Partnership (P3) Schools in Nova Scotia" (Halifax, NS: Atlantic Institute for Market Studies, 2017).

9   Canada Ministry of Finance, "2023 Fall Economic Statement," Fall 2023, canada.ca.

10 Ontario Ministry of Finance, "2023 Ontario Economic Outlook and Fiscal Review – Building a Stronger Ontario Together" (Ottawa: King's Printer for Ontario, November 2023).

11 Ammar Al-Joundi, Rene Amirault, George Armoyan, Louis Audet, Pascale Audette, Jim Balsillie, Ross Beaty, et al, "Open Letter to the Minister of Finance of Canada and Provincial Finance Ministers," March 4, 2024, lba.ca.

12 Ontario Teachers' Pension Plan, "Statement on Ontario Infrastructure Bank," November 2, 2023, otpp.com.

13 Evan Siddall, "Federal Government Should Not Be Pushing Pension Funds to Invest More in Canada," *Globe and Mail*, November 24, 2023.

14 D. Stiff and P. Smetanin, "OMERS and Its Members: Ontario Economic Contribution 2020" (Toronto: Canadian Centre for Economic Analysis, October 2021).

15 OMERS, "OMERS Impact: Economic Contribution and Social Value," 2022.

16 George Parker, Jim Pickard, and Gill Plimmer, "UK Water Sector Faces Biggest Crisis since Thatcher's 1989 Privatisation," *Financial Times*, June 28, 2023, ft.com.

17 Jessica Shankleman and Eamon Farhat, "Thames Water Faces 100 Million Penalty for Missed Targets," *Bloomberg*, September 26, 2023, bloomberg.com.

18 Ronan Martin and Jessica Shankleman, "Thames Water Pays Up for First Bond since Industry Chaos," *Bloomberg*, October 18, 2023, bloomberg.com.

19 Miles Brignall, "Thames Water Told by Auditors It Could Run out of Money by April," *The Guardian*, December 3, 2023, theguardian.com.

20 Helena Horton, "Thames Water Pumped at Least 72bn Litres of Sewage into Thames since 2020," *The Guardian*, November 10, 2023, theguardian.com.

21 Brignall, "Thames Water Told by Auditors."

22 Gill Plimmer, "Thames Water to Be Investigated over Financial Stability and Dividends," *Financial Times*, December 5, 2023, ft.com.

23 Helena Horton, "Thames Water Urged to 'Get a Grip' on Testing Water Supply after Illness Outbreak," *The Guardian*, May 29, 2024, theguardian.com.

24 Julius Melnitzer, "Why Big Pension Funds Love Australian Ports," *Benefits Canada*, March 21, 2017, benefitscanada.com.

25 Deborah Cowen, *The Deadly Life of Logistics: Mapping Violence in Global Trade* (Minneapolis: University of Minnesota Press, 2014).

26 OMERS, "OMERS Infrastructure Announces Investment in BridgeTex," August 21, 2018, omers.com.

27 Heritage Royalty, "About Heritage: History," 2023, heritageroyalty.ca.

28 Ontario Teachers' Pension Plan, *Annual Responsible Investing and Climate Strategy Report*, 2021.

29 OMERS, *2016 Annual Report*, 2017, 35.

30 LAVCA Venture Investors, "OMERS Announces First Direct Infrastructure Investment in South America," April 11, 2017, lavca.org.

31 CBC News Alerts (@cbcalerts), "Brazil's new president elect, Jair Bolsonaro, is a right-winger who leans towards more open markets. This could mean fresh opportunities for Canadian companies looking to invest in the resource-rich country," Twitter, October 28, 2018, twitter.com.

32 Tom Fraser, "Canadian Pension Funds Driving Privatization in Brazil," *Canadian Dimension*, September 14, 2021, canadiandimension.com.

33 Canada Pension Plan Investment Board, "CPP Investments Net Assets Total $539 Billion at 2022 Fiscal Year-End" (Newswire, May 19, 2022), newswire.ca.

34 Bloomberg News, "Canada's Top Pension Fund among 'Big Boys' Setting Sights on India's US $1.9 Trillion Economy," *Financial Post*, December 4, 2014, financialpost.com.

35 John Tilak and Euan Rocha, "India's Modi Courts Canadian Banks, Insurers, Pension Funds," *Reuters*, April 16, 2015, reuters.com.

36 Thomson Reuters, "Canada's Pension Fund Ready to Invest

$2b in Affordable Housing in India, Official Says," *CBC*, November 1, 2015, cbc.ca.

37 "India Courting Canada's Pension Funds for Infrastructure Investments," *Benefits Canada*, March 15, 2022, benefitscanada.com.

38 Pranab Bardhan, "The 'New' India: A Political Economic Diagnosis," *New Left Review*, no. 136 (August 2022): 6–7.

39 Ontario Teachers' Pension Plan, "Ontario Teachers' Invests Further in National Highways Infra Trust in India," October 12, 2022, otpp.com.

40 OMERS, "OMERS Announces First Infrastructure Investment in India," February 22, 2019, omers.com.

41 Ontario Teachers' Pension Plan, "Mahindra Group and Ontario Teachers' to Form a Strategic Partnership in the Renewable Energy Space," September 17, 2022, otpp.com.

42 Azure Power, "OMERS Infrastructure Purchases 19.4% Stake in Azure Power Global Ltd," August 6, 2021, azurepower.com.

43 Ontario Teachers' Pension Plan, "Ontario Teachers' Announce Agreement to Acquire a Significant Majority Stake in Sahyadri Hospitals from the Everstone Group," August 16, 2022, otpp.com.

44 Ontario Teachers' Pension Plan, "Ontario Teachers' Grows Presence in India with Establishment of Mumbai Office," September 27, 2022, otpp.com.

45 Ontario Teachers' Pension Plan, "Investment Opportunities across India," 2023, otpp.com.

46 Ontario Teachers' Pension Plan, "National Highways Infra Trust."

47 Layan Odeh and Ben Bartenstein, "Ontario Teachers' $181 Billion Pension Fund Pauses Private China Deals," *Bloomberg*, January 31, 2023.

48 Mary McDougall, Ellesheva Kissin, and Kate Duguid, "Israel Raises $6bn in Borrowing Bonanza to Fund War against Hamas," *Financial Times*, November 17, 2023, ft.com.

49 Kunal Chaudhary, "Canadian Pension Funds Invested 1.6 Billion in Companies Tied to Israeli Apartheid," *The Breach*, January 16, 2024, breachmedia.ca.

50 "CPPIB Investment in War Crimes and Potentially Genocide Increases to over 16 B in 2024," Just Peace Advocates, 2024, justpeaceadvocates.ca.

51 "No Profits from Palestinian Deaths: Ontario Teachers Demand Pension Plan Divestment from Israeli War Crimes," World Beyond War, worldbeyondwar.org.

52 Kwame Nkrumah, *Neo-Colonialism: The Last Stage of Imperialism*, reprinted (London: Panaf, 2004), xiii.

53 Tom Fraser, "The Politics of Pipelines Were the Politics of Canadian Sovereignty," *Globe and Mail*, June 22, 2018, theglobeandmail.com.

54 Gunnar Adler-Karlsson and Abraham Rotstein, *Reclaiming the Canadian Economy: A Swedish Approach through Functional Socialism* (Toronto: House of Anansi Press, 1970).

55 Steven C. High, *Industrial Sunset: The Making of North America's Rust Belt, 1969–1984* (Toronto: University of Toronto Press, 2003).

56 CBC Ideas, "Extracting Justice: The Human Rights Impact of Canadian Mining around the World," May 30, 2023, cbc.ca.

57 Cowen, *Deadly Life of Logistics*, 14.

58 "Today, the Provincial Government Announced Plans to Create an 'Arms-Length and Board-Governed' Ontario Infrastructure Bank...," LinkedIn, *Shift Action for Pension Wealth and Planet Health* (blog), November 2023, linkedin.com.

59 "PSE to Build Montana Wind Farm as Coal-Fired Energy Winds Down," LinkedIn, *Shift Action for Pension Wealth and Planet Health* (blog), December 8, 2023, linkedin.com.

60 "Three of Canada's Largest Pension Funds...," LinkedIn, *Shift Action for Pension Wealth and Planet Health* (blog), August 2023, linkedin.com.

61 Bardhan, "The 'New' India," 7.

62 SHIFT—Action for Pension Wealth and Planet Health. linkedin.com.

63 SHIFT–Action for Pension Wealth and Planet Health, "Thames Water–a Cautionary Tale for 'Responsible Investors' and Privatized Utilities," July 11, 2023, shiftaction.ca.

64 Tom Fraser, "Only Labor Can Force Canadian Pension Funds to Divest from Oil," *Jacobin*, October 19, 2021, jacobin.com.

65 Jeremy Rifkin and Randy Barber, *The North Will Rise Again: Pensions, Politics and Power in the 1980s* (Boston: Beacon Press, 1978).

66 Jack Quarter, *Crossing the Line: Unionized Employee Ownership and Investment Funds* (Toronto: James Lorimer, 1995).

67 Quarter, *Crossing the Line*, 214.

68 Tessa Hebb, "Introduction" in *Working Capital: The Power of Labor's Pensions*, eds. Archon Fung, Tessa Hebb, and Joel Rogers (Ithaca, NY: ILR Press, 2001), 1.

69 Kevin Breuninger, "Ron DeSantis Calls for 'Crippling the ESG Movement' in New Book," *CNBC*, February 28, 2023, cnbc.com.

70 Jon Entine, ed., *Pension Fund Politics: The Dangers of Socially Responsible Investing* (Washington, D.C: AEI Press, 2005).

71 CUPE Ontario, "Not Just 'One Tough Year': The Need for a Review of OMERS Investment Performance," May, 2021.

72 Cowen, *Deadly Life of Logistics*, 8.

CONCLUSION: BUILDING A JUST CITY, BUILDING A JUST RETIREMENT

1 Frank N. Marrocco, "Ontario's Long Term Care COVID 19 Commission" (Toronto: Long-Term Care COVID19 Commission, April 2021), 13, 16.

2 André Picard, *Neglected No More: The Urgent Need to Improve the Lives of Canada's Elders in the Wake of a Pandemic* (Toronto: Random House Canada, 2021).

3 Kevin Skerrett, "The Pension Fund Profiteers Are Making a Killing from Long-Term Care," *Jacobin*, January 12, 2021; "Public Sector Union Pressuring PSP to 'Pull Out' of Long-Term Care Investments," *Benefits Canada*, December 14, 2020.

4 "Teachers' to Acquire Amica Mature Lifestyles," *Benefits Canada*, September 2, 2015.

5 Albertina Torsoli, "Orpea HQ, Nursing Homes Searched in 'Gravediggers' Scandal," *Bloomberg*, February 15, 2022, bloomberg.com; "CPPIB-Backed European Care Home Operator Faces Allegations of Elder Abuse, Misappropriation of Public Money," *Benefits Canada*, March 1, 2022.

6 Ontario Coalition Against Poverty, "OCAP Statement Regarding Encampment Clearing at Trinity Bellwoods," June 22, 2021, web.archive.org.

7 "Survey Finds 44% of Institutional Investors Likely to

Increase Allocations to Alternatives," *Benefits Canada*, December 13, 2022, benefitscanada.com.

8   Neil Brenner, Peter Marcuse, and Margit Mayer, eds., *Cities for People, Not for Profit: Critical Urban Theory and the Right to the City* (New York: Routledge, 2012).

9   David Harvey, *Rebel Cities: From the Right to the City to the Urban Revolution* (London: Verso, 2012).

10   Shannon O'Neil, "Chile's Failed Pensions Are Neoliberalism's Badge of Shame," *Bloomberg*, July 28, 2022, bloomberg.com.

11   Bill Tufts and Lee Fairbanks, *Pension Ponzi: How Public Sector Unions Are Bankrupting Canada's Health Care, Education and Your Retirement* (Etobicoke, ON: J. Wiley & Sons Canada, 2011).

12   Martin Lukacs and Emma Paling, "The Inside Story of How Education Workers Beat Back Doug Ford," *The Breach*, December 14, 2022, breachmedia.ca.

13   Tom Fraser, "Canadian Pension Funds Driving Privatization in Brazil," *Canadian Dimension*, September 14, 2021, canadiandimension.com.

14   Amalgamated Clothing Workers of America, "Proceedings of the Eighth Biennial Convention of the Amalgamated Clothing Workers of America, Held in Cincinnati, May 14-19, 1928," 1928, 116.

INDEX

TOM FRASER is a union researcher based in Tkaranto/ Toronto. With an academic background in labour history, his research focuses narrowly on Ontario's long-term care sector and more broadly on deindustrial political economy. His writing on labour, pensions, and infrastructure policy has appeared in *Jacobin*, *Canadian Dimension*, and *The Globe and Mail*.